My Beloved Miami Dolphins

My Beloved MIAMI Dolphins

From the Perspective of a Lifelong Fan

ROMAIN DUFOUR III

ReadersMagnet, LLC

My Beloved Miami Dolphins: From the Perspective of a Lifelong Fan
Copyright © 2024 by Romain DuFour lll

Published in the United States of America
ISBN   Paperback: 979-8-89091-545-0
ISBN   eBook: 979-8-89091-546-7

All rights reserved. No part of this publication may be reproduced, stored in a retrieval system or transmitted in any way by any means, electronic, mechanical, photocopy, recording or otherwise without the prior permission of the author except as provided by USA copyright law.

The opinions expressed by the author are not necessarily those of ReadersMagnet, LLC.

ReadersMagnet, LLC
10620 Treena Street, Suite 230 | San Diego, California, 92131 USA
1.619. 354. 2643 | www.readersmagnet.com

Book design copyright © 2024 by ReadersMagnet, LLC. All rights reserved.

Cover design by Jhie Oraiz
Interior design by Dorothy Lee

TABLE OF CONTENTS

Chapter 1: "The Year Of 1984" 7

Chapter 2: The Consistent Years 24

Chapter 3: The Shula Effect 41

Chapter 4: Heartbreaking Losses 58

Chapter 5: The Search To Replace Dan Marino 76

Chapter 6: The Lost Years 93

Chapter 7: The Bridesmaids Of The A.f.c. East 110

Chapter 8: Dolphins New Era 128

Chapter 9: The Dolphins Should Have Motivation To Win 145

Chapter 10: Are The Days Of Glory Ahead? 162

Chapter 11: Memorable Wins 179

CHAPTER 1
"The Year of 1984"

My love affair with the Miami Dolphins commenced in 1984. I was a ten-year old kid in the sixth grade. On opening day of the 1984 NFL regular season, the Miami Dolphins game against the Washington Redskins set the tone for a season of fun and excitement. The black and white twenty inch RCA television that I had during that time, prominently showed the long touchdown pass from the second year quarterback, Dan Marino to wide receiver, Mark Duper. At that very instant, my life-long love of the Miami Dolphins commenced. There was a young, handsome, curly-haired quarterback who looked similar to the actor, David Hasselhoff, who played on hit the television show, during that time, called ", Knight Rider".

Marino's long flowing locks would flow effortlessly in the back of his helmet when he threw a touchdown pass to his speedy wide-receiver core. Each football game during that 1984 season for the Miami Dolphins featured a plethora of offensive excitement. In the former Orange Bowl Stadium in Miami, Florida, I can vividly recall the tall palm trees that were in back of the scoreboard, which would blow from side to side each time there was a South Florida breeze.

Though, there were twenty-seven other teams that played in the National Football League during that time, no other team captured the fun and excitement of football like the

Marino lead, Dolphins. I did not know much about football in the genesis of the 1984 season, but at the end of it, my football knowledge would drastically increase, due to the Dolphins' offensive power. The catalyst to the Dolphins offense was none other than, Dan Marino.

Each offensive play commences with the quarterback, and Marino's talent shined as brightly as the Florida sun. Coming out of the University of Pittsburgh in 1983, Marino displayed his talent throughout his entire college career, but in his senior year, he and his college team did not have the year that they anticipated and hoped for. Although, Marino was deemed talented by the consensus of coaches and talent scouts in the N.F.L., he was the last quarterback taken in the first-round of the 1983 draft.

The Miami Dolphins did not know that the quarterback who slid down to them in the 1983 draft would have the type of year that he had in his second season. In 1984, Marino threw for a then record, 48 touchdowns and 5,084 passing yards, which stood for many years after his subsequent retirement at the end of the 1999 season. 1984, was the year of Dan Marino.

He won the award for Most Valuable Player during that year, and his influence in the Dolphins organization, as well as league wide, catapulted him into one of the young faces of the N.F.L. The Dolphins adapted their playing style from a run-oriented, balanced team to primarily a pass- oriented team. It was Dan Marino's golden arm that would thrust the Dolphins' organization into the national spotlight, and help the team to become one of the most exciting offenses in the National Football League.

Dan Marino could not enjoy being one of the most gifted quarterbacks in the 1984 season on his own. His receiving core during that time, which consisted of Mark Duper, Mark Clayton, Nat Moore, Jimmy Cefalo, Bruce Hardy, Joe Rose, and Dan Johnson provided the hands that received many of

Marino's strong-armed passes. The speedy receivers, Mark Duper and Mark Clayton were instrumental in the Dolphins' offensive fire- power. Week after week during the 1984 season, the trio of Dan Marino, Mark Duper, and Mark Clayton were always on the highlight reels during that season. Both receivers, who stood at 5'9 inches became affectionately known as, the "Marks Brothers". Duper and Clayton always had a friendly competition to become Marino's leading receiving target.

I believe that due to this competitive drive for both men, the Dolphins' receiving core became one of the elite receiving corps in the entire league in 1984. As a fan during that season, it was exciting to see two receivers who were considered diminutive by professional football standards thrive and succeed. I can recall thinking as a child that the "Marks Brothers" gave many children around the nation hope that a small to average height individual can succeed in playing a "big man's game."

Though, the Marks Brothers, Duper and Clayton, were not the biggest individuals, both exhibited brute strength and toughness. They were not just speedy and fast, but they were also strong throughout their whole bodies. Mark Duper and Clayton had world-class speed, especially Duper, who ran track in his younger days.

Clayton, on the other hand, was deceptively blessed with the strength of a burly, offensive lineman. It was amazing to see an individual who was considered small by many in the National Football League prove that he belonged in spite of his stature. Once Duper and Clayton's receiving talents became displayed throughout the 1984 season, they too, would enjoy national recognition.

Defenses could not stop Marino, Duper, and Clayton for almost the whole entire season of 1984. The Marks Brothers, with their special individual talents, became the example of how wide receivers who were less than 6'0 tall, could also enjoy success in the league, as much as their larger counterparts.

Duper and Clayton were just as much responsible for the success of the Miami Dolphins during the 1984 campaign as quarterback, Dan Marino was.

As I reflect back on the 1984 season of the Miami Dolphins, it was a season filled with excitement and anticipation. I can recall how I could not wait to see the Dolphins play on Sundays during that particular year because they started out the season winning their first eleven games. There was a period during that season that I thought that the Dolphins could rival another Dolphins team, which were the unprecedented 1972 Dolphins. Personally, I did not know about the 72' undefeated Dolphins before the 1984 season because ironically I was born in the following Super Bowl winning season of 1973. Also, I was just a young boy and a new fan of the National Football League. Marino and the Marks Brothers proved in the 1984 season that winning could become fun and infectious.

In the 1980s, offensive styles commence to change. Most teams in the decades prior to the decade of the 1980s relied upon a sound running game. Teams like the 1960s Green Bay Packers and Cleveland Browns won the majority of their games with that particular style.

For the Miami Dolphins, prior to the 1984 season, they were winning with a potent running attack. The Dolphins of the 1970s won primarily with the legs of Hall of Fame fullback, Larry Csonka, and halfbacks Mercury Morris, and Jim Kiick. When these players left the organization, after their playing days, the Dolphins transitioned into more of a balanced attack.

Legendary Hall of Fame and Super Bowl winning quarterback, Bob Griese played his entire career with the Miami Dolphins from 1967-1980. During the years that he played, he was not known for throwing bombs like his divisional rival, former New York Jet and Hall of Fame quarterback, Joe Namath. Though Griese enjoyed pass catchers, such as,

Paul Warfield, the Dolphins prior to Marino's arrival were not known for scoring 50- yard touchdowns through passing.

Their primary offensive attack was moving the chains and methodically advancing the ball downfield. Before the Marino era commenced in 1983, the Miami Dolphins were not known primarily for their offense. Good defense and a solid running game was the primary way that the Dolphins won the majority of their games in the 1970s and early 1980s.

Many of the Dolphin fans prior to Dan Marino's arrival did not have any clue that the brand of football that they have grown to become accustomed to would dramatically change. Quarterbacks Don Strock and David Woodley were not known for throwing long touchdown passes. They managed to help the Dolphins get to Super Bowl XVII after the 1982 regular season.

Though Strock and Woodley were talented enough to manage the Dolphins passing attack, they did not have as much talent and arm ability as quarterback, Dan Marino. When the Dolphins fans of that era learned about the drafting of Marino, I do not know if they envisioned an offense that was "bombs away." In a 1983 regular season loss against their AFC East, division rival, the Buffalo Bills, Marino displayed glimpses of what his sophomore season of 1984 would be like.

The Dolphins made the playoffs in 1983, but after Marino took the helm, 1984 was a season for the organization and fans, which would become one of the franchise's most memorable seasons yet. Marino throwing long touchdown passes to Duper and Clayton became a normal sight and experience for fans. It also marked the beginning of the Dan Marino national phenomenon.

Some fans of professional football might not have been Dolphins fans, but after seeing the second year quarterback dominate the National Football League during that year with his long touchdown passes each week, his legend grew into superstardom. The comparisons to former New York Jets quarterback, Joe Namath, became more prevalent among fans and league officials because of Marino's cannon of an arm. Touchdowns and bombs in the 1984 season eventually became synonymous with the Miami Dolphins franchise.

Offensive football became one of the contributing factors of why the National Football League grew in television audiences and attendance in the 1980s. Teams like the San Diego Chargers, now playing in Los Angeles, and the Miami Dolphins played a style of football that appealed to the average fan. There is not anything more exciting in watching a football game than seeing a quarterback launch a football 60-yards in the air to the waiting arms and hands of a wide receiver ready to catch the ball.

When I would watch the Dolphins games on television as a young lad in the 1984 season, I can still recall the stands in the Orange Bowl being packed with excited fans. The excited Dolphins fans were there to see Marino and the Marks Brothers score a plethora of points and offensive touchdowns threw the air. I learned that offense does bring fans into the stands, but defense is responsible for winning championships.

It is a beautiful sight to see offensive football at its best. In 1984, the Dolphins passing offense was tops in the National Football league that year. Previously, in 1983, the Dolphins offense could not boast that ranking.

Thanks to the trio of Marino, Duper, and Clayton, the Dolphins franchise enjoyed one of the best offensive passing ranks in franchise history. Mark Clayton set a then record for pass receiving touchdowns with 18. The 1984 season also marked the beginning of a prolific passing touchdown combination between Marino and Clayton. Although, the passing combination of Marino to Clayton was lethal to opposing defenses, the combination of Marino to Duper was also dominant.

With the emergence of Dan Marino, Mark Duper and Mark Clayton on the Miami Dolphins offensive side of the ball, all of them became household names not only in the local Miami-Dade County and Broward area, but in 1984, they all would be linked together during that season and also in the succession of years to come. As a Dolphins fan in the 1984 season, it seemed as though the offense of the Dolphins could score a passing touchdown at will. The offense during that season did not have to worry about getting first downs.

Scoring became second nature for the Dolphins in 1984. Now the running game was not featured prominently on offense because that unit had the three young stars in the passing attack. I can recall how during the 1984 campaign how Marino, Duper, and Clayton basically carried the whole team that year.

Because of the influence of these young stars, the Miami Dolphins became an attraction and a sensation throughout the once run-dominant league. The Dolphins demonstrated to the league, as well as fans nationwide that a team can become victorious and successful with a trio of passing talent. Though, the team finished with a 14-2 record, the team became the premier team in the A.F.C. (American Football Conference). What I gathered from the 1984 season is that the young passing trio of the Dolphins would be one to become reckoned with, due to their talent, heart, and passion.

Football can be a brutal game. It is a sport that does not welcome finesse. In the 1980s, the game of football was not played with the three yards and a cloud of dust mentality. With the rules change of 1978, which introduced what is commonly referred to as pass interference, offensive football would commence to change.

Before the 1978 rules change which favored defenses, football was a game that was played with the mentality that anything goes. For example, defensive backs and linebackers could jam the wide receivers at the line of scrimmage before the receivers were able to run their passing routes. When the wide receiver did get a chance to run down the field, the receiver could be hit and knocked down before the football had a chance to reach the pass catcher.

Teams like the Oakland Raiders and Pittsburgh Steelers benefited and thrived on that brand of football that was played in the 1970s that favored bone- crushing hits. If the average fan of the 1970s and previous decades, loved to see hard-hitters on defense deliver hard hits, like the Oakland Raiders' defensive back Jack Tatum, or the Pittsburgh Steelers' defensive nightmares, defensive back Mel Blount and linebacker Jack Lambert, hit wide receivers down the field and impede their routes, football in the 1980s was beginning to favor the quarterback and wide receiver tandems instead. After the rules change of 1978 became official, which was primarily due to Pittsburgh Steelers defensive back, Mel Blount's dominance at the line of scrimmage against wide receivers who were not able to run routes, or catch a pass down field because of Blount's intimidation and hard hitting persistence, pass interference was a rule that had to become implemented.

Teams that had a strong armed quarterback, such as, the Miami Dolphins with quarterback, Dan Marino, were now able to complete 50 yard passes down the field without becoming too concerned about whether or not the wide receiver's routes would become impeded due to an overaggressive defensive player. In the 1984 season, alone, many teams who had a reliable quarterback and receiving tandem were "flying high" because of the defense not becoming able to impose their will on offenses. Do not mistake me. Football was still played aggressively on the defensive side of the ball with hard-hitting players, such as, the New York Giants, Hall of Fame linebacker, Lawrence Taylor and San Francisco 49ers Hall of Fame defensive back, Ronnie Lott, who also invoked fear into opposing offenses.

The Miami Dolphins offense for the majority of the 1984 season made football look easy and effortless. Fans during that season could not take a long snack break because Marino, Duper, and Clayton were too busy throwing and receiving touchdown passes, which could be scored anywhere on the field, quickly and immediately. During that magical regular season in 1984, as a young fan, I thought to myself that football is not so difficult to play and watch. Before the 1984 season, I was more interested in music and playing video games, but the 1984 Dolphins changed my perception of football with their effortless offensive play.

As a young Miami Dolphins fan, in the regular season of the 1984 campaign, I viewed the Dolphins as a dominant team, especially, in the A.F.C. (American Football Conference). During that year, the Dolphins had a perfect record against every divisional opponent. In fact, the team's divisional record was 8-0.

The Los Angeles Raiders and the San Diego Chargers were the only losses that the 1984 Miami Dolphins would suffer. The first loss against the Dan Fouts lead Chargers was a memorable overtime defeat. I can recall how both teams during that year had offensive fire- power.

That game was built up to be a game between the young upstart in Dan Marino versus the explosive air attack of Dan Fouts and offensive guru, coach Don "air" Coryell. I was excited and curious to see what Marino and the Marks Brothers could do against an offense, which was their "mirror image." Though, the Dolphins lost a hard fought battle against the Chargers, I still considered the Dolphins a dominant team in the A.F.C. Conference.

A couple of weeks later, the Dolphins would also lose a second and final loss of the regular season, which was against the Marcus Allen lead, Los Angeles Raiders. This game was high scoring, and I can vividly remember how running back, Marcus Allen ran wild against the Dolphins' defense on that particular day. Although, the Dolphins suffered their second loss in two weeks, I knew in the back of my young mind that they were still good enough to reach the Super Bowl.

I can recall on the long running football show, "Inside the N.F.L., a 1984 interview with some of the Dolphins players discussing the potential of becoming another Dolphin team with a chance of ending the season undefeated. From week 7 of that year, I can recall how the undefeated record became a topic of discussion. It was during those interviews that I learned about the Miami Dolphins' undefeated 1972 season, as well as the teams' winning culture and tradition.

In my mind, the only team that I believe would pose a challenge to my beloved Miami Dolphins in the 1984 campaign in the A.F.C. was the Allen lead, Raiders. I also knew that the Seattle Seahawks, with Hall of Fame wide receiver, Steve Largent, as well as quarterback, Dave Krieg were also dangerous. The Los Angeles Raiders just won Super Bowl XVIII the previous year.

Because the Dolphins were the class of the American Football Conference in that year by earning the A.F.C. East title, as well as the conference's best record, they would enjoy a week off, and eventually play the winner of the A.F.C. Wild Card game. Whoever survived that Wild Card game would ultimately have to face the Dolphins in the Divisional Playoff game, in the hostile environment of the famed Orange Bowl in Miami, home of the young, talented, offensive-explosive Miami Dolphins. The mindset of the Dolphins was revenge for either team that they would have to face in the Divisional round of the 1984 playoffs.

Seattle won a defensive battle against the Los Angeles Raiders. So the Dolphins did not have to avenge their regular season loss against the Raiders. The stakes were high in the match-up between the Seattle Seahawks and the Miami Dolphins. This was a chance for the winner of the Divisional Playoff game to reach the A.F.C. Championship, therefore becoming one game away from the ultimate game, Super Bowl XIX. In 1983, the Miami Dolphins suffered a surprising loss in the playoffs at home against the Seattle Seahawks. It was definitely an upset because the Dolphins were the favorite to win that game.

The Seahawks had to travel thousands of miles across the opposite end of the country to play in the Orange Bowl, which was home field advantage for the Dolphins for several years. Also, prior to the 1983 season, the Miami Dolphins were the runner-ups in Super Bowl XVII against the John Riggins lead, Washington Redskins. The Dolphins expected to reach another A.F.C. Championship game, as well as another chance to avenge their Super Bowl loss.

Again it was déjà vu all over again for the Miami Dolphins in the 1984 A.F.C. playoffs. The Seahawks were a formidable opponent due to their sound running attack and passing attack of quarterback, Dave Krieg. What ensued after the first half of that 1984 Divisional Playoff game was total domination of the Marino lead, Dolphins.

Personally, I knew that if the Dolphins could survive and avenge their 1983 playoff loss against the Seattle Seahawks, I knew that a Super Bowl berth was on the horizon. They did it. It was a shaky first quarter for the league's most potent offense when they were held scoreless in the first quarter, but in the second quarter and beyond, the Dolphins never looked back.

Miami's defense played complimentary football as the Dolphins were finally able to seek revenge with a 31-10 win over the Seahawks. What I can recall the most from that game was how breezy the weather was. I remember when Mark Clayton scored his touchdown against the Seahawk defense how trash from the stands were following him into the end zone.

When the Dolphins were able to make it to the A.F.C. Championship game, as a fan I did not have any concerns. The opponent who the Dolphins would face would be none other than the Pittsburgh Steelers, the team that dominated the 1970s. It was also Marino's hometown team who did not consider him a worthy draft pick in the 1983 draft.

The Steelers could have easily drafted Marino in the 1983 draft because they knew so much about his family and background, by him spending all of his educational years in the city of Pittsburgh. From birth to young adulthood, Marino was a likely candidate to carry on the Steelers tradition. For whatever unknown reason, Marino would not become the quarterback to succeed legendary and Hall of Fame quarterback, Terry Bradshaw. I can only imagine how being snubbed by his hometown franchise gave Marino the incentive and motivation to win this game in particular.

Sunshine filled the air in the Orange Bowl on Sunday, January 6, 1985. I can still hear the voices of Hall of Fame radio commentator, the late great Dick Enberg, as well as Hall of Fame Los Angeles Rams defensive tackle, the late great Merlin Olsen lending their voices in commentary. The A.F.C. Championship game between the Pittsburgh Steelers and Miami Dolphins would mark the Dolphins finest game in the Marino era.

The young talented trio of Marino, Duper, and Clayton were basically unstoppable in that game. Each had a hand in many of the Dolphins' scoring opportunities on that day. Many fans of the National Football League had expectations that the Dolphins would prevail over the Mark Malone and John Stallworth led Steelers.

In 1984, the Pittsburgh Steelers were a team in transition. Gone, were stars like, Hall of Fame quarterback, Terry Bradshaw, and Hall of Fame wide receiver, Lynn Swann. Wide receiver John Stallworth and legendary Steelers safety, Donnie Shell, were just a few of the remaining original members left from the Steelers' dynasties of the 1970s. It seemed during that game that there would be a changing of the guard, in regard to the team who would reign supreme in the A.F.C.

After the Dolphins 45-28 win over the mighty Pittsburgh Steelers, many assumed that the Dolphins would be one of the teams at the forefront of A.F.C. supremacy. Marino and his talented receiving core could not be stopped in two dominant wins over relatively good football teams. The road to Super Bowl XIX in the 1984-85 season was a smooth one for the high-octane Dolphins.

The Miami Dolphins passing offense, especially, Marino, Duper, and Clayton was special and talented. Their talent alone became both the admiration and envy of the entire National Football League. Fans wanted to see them each week, while their peers wanted to end their successful season.

Smiles, sunshine, and touchdowns described the Dolphins talented passing trio. When those two A.F.C. playoff games was won in dominant fashion by the Dolphins, the consensus around the N.F.L., was mostly ready to crown the Miami Dolphins as world champions. Over in the N.F.C. (National Football Conference), there were a plethora of talented and solid football teams.

The Washington Redskins had an approximately three-year reign in that particular conference by winning Super Bowl XVII over the Miami Dolphins, while also making the big game the next year, which resulted in a loss to the eventual Super Bowl Champions, the Los Angeles Raiders. In 1981, a new team was emerging into the spotlight in the N.F.C. After the 49ers won Super Bowl XVI after the 1981 season, they did have one lean year. In 1984, the San Francisco 49ers were again primed to challenge for another Super Bowl with a 15-1 record. The team was led by the late great Hall of Fame San Francisco 49er coach, Bill Walsh and legendary Hall of Fame quarterback, Joe Montana.

Brewing in the 1984-85 N.F.L. playoffs was a Super Bowl game between two young quarterbacks who would go on to become the faces of the National Football League, and two coaches who would enjoy coaching success. The Don Shula 14-2 Dolphins would eventually face the 15-1 Bill Walsh 49ers in one of the most anticipated Super Bowls during that time in the game's history.

Super Bowl XIX was one of the most anticipated Super Bowls in the modern Super Bowl era. It was played on January 20, 1985 on the Stanford campus in Palo Alto, California. The match-up between Dan Marino and the Dolphins and Joe Montana of the 49ers was advertised as basically an even match.

The 49ers were playing the game in their own backyard. I can remember how I felt before that game. My thoughts were that it was not fair to play a Super Bowl, just miles away from the team's home stadium.

For the Miami Dolphins, some critics commenced to be concern for the defensive unit. It was Marino's high-powered offense versus the 49ers that was a team of balance and completion. In my young mind, I never thought that the Dolphins' offense on that day would be stopped.

In an interview on the weekly football series, "Inside the N.F.L., I can vividly recollect an interview they did with Dolphins' pro bowl wide receiver, Mark Clayton. Paraphrasing from that interview, Clayton was asked how he thought the game would turn out. He said," I think it would be a game that would be until the last man."

Immediately when Clayton uttered that quote, which I am paraphrasing, I anticipated in my eleven-year old mind that the game would end in dramatic fashion. In other words, the team that had the football last, on the last offensive possession would be the victor. With the Dolphins offense averaging 38 points in the two previous playoff games, I thought that the high scoring trend would continue.

In the first quarter of Super Bowl XIX, it started in the Miami Dolphins' favor. After the quarter ended, Marino and the Dolphins held a 10-7 lead over the 49ers. The game seemed like it would become another high scoring game for the Marino lead, Miami Dolphins.

When the 49ers scored a barrage of points in the second quarter of that Super Bowl, which was 21 points, I must admit that I began to have concern that the Dolphins would have a difficult hill to climb. The other individual who I was watching that game with tried to reassure me that the Dolphins would eventually come back from their halftime deficit.

Each time that I tried to become optimistic that the Dolphins would mount a comeback in that all- important game, my optimism turned into sadness. Marino was sacked 4 times by the 49ers' defense. This was the most times that he was sacked by a single opponent that whole entire season.

The eventual Hall of Fame quarterback was only sacked 13 times in the 1984 season, which was remarkable for a quarterback in only his second season. In Super Bowl XIX, that was the first time that I had seen the all-pro quarterback rattled and out of sync. Bill Walsh and his defensive staff had a defensive game plan that confused the young star with a defensive coverage that consisted of a plethora of defensive backs. Due to that game plan, the Dolphins talented receiving core could not get open on their routes because of the 49ers defensive backs' blanketed coverage.

At the end of Super Bowl XIX, the Dolphins would not gain a victory. The game was eventually lop-sided, with the San Francisco 49ers winning decisively, 38-16. I do not like to revert back to that particular game because it symbolizes deep sadness for me as a loyal, Miami Dolphins fan.

My mindset after that disappointing defeat was that the Dolphins would be a team that could challenge for the Super Bowl, again. I still remember the Diet Pepsi commercial when Dan Marino told San Francisco 49ers quarterback, Joe Montana that he was "buying the Pepsi, next year." Marino was giving all Dolphins fans like me hope that he and the team would return to the big game, the following year.

There was not any doubt in my mind that the Miami Dolphins were likely to return to the Super Bowl and battle for their third world championship. The Dolphins were runner-ups in two previous Super Bowl games in approximately a three- year span. I thought to myself that my Dolphins are at least due for one Super Bowl title.

The dream of the Dolphins acquiring their third world championship in franchise history was not meant to be on that cool foggy day in Palo Alto, California in January of 1985. I still remember how emotional I was after the Dolphins' damaging Super Bowl defeat. Seeing Marino sacked that many times in a game, and Duper and Clayton not being able to experience a touchdown catch in the Super Bowl, after a record-breaking season until that point, was heartbreaking.

When the 1984 season was completed, the Dolphins still had a team of all-pros and pro-bowlers. Dan Marino was an all-pro that year, and the list of other Dolphin pro-bowlers included wide receivers, Mark Duper and Mark Clayton, offensive linemen, center, Dwight Stephenson and guard, Ed Newman. On defense, the pro-bowl talent from the 1984 Dolphins included defensive linemen, Bob Baumhower and linebacker and pass rush specialist, A.J. Duhe. Rounding out the pro-bowl selections for the Miami Dolphins in that magical season was punter, Reggie Roby.

The Dolphins organization has not been able to experience that many pro-bowl selections, since. After the 1984 season, no one could tell me that Super Bowl XIX would become the Dolphin franchise's last Super Bowl appearance, and also the talented offensive trio of Marino, Duper, and Clayton's last and only chance to become Super Bowl champions. Years of offensive prowess and consistency would ensue for the Dolphins franchise in the Marino, Duper, and Clayton era.

Though, 1984 would become a season of enjoyable memories for the most part for Dolphins fans, the Super Bowl loss ultimately revealed how unbalanced the Dolphins' offense really was. It took many years for the Miami Dolphins to experience a 1000- yard rusher. Sure, the Dolphins were exciting to watch from 1984 until Duper and Clayton's departures after the 1992 season, but becoming a complete team on offense and defense, while also becoming balanced on offense would be what the aqua and orange nation would spend many decades in search of.

CHAPTER 2
The Consistent Years

Throughout the decade of the 1970s, the Miami Dolphins emerged as one of the N.F.L.'s elite teams. The Dolphins could be mentioned in the same winning category as teams such as, the Dallas Cowboys, Pittsburgh Steelers, and Oakland Raiders. In that decade, the Dolphins would win the A.F.C. East divisional title five times.

From 1970-2000, the Dolphins would make the playoffs 21 times during that span. For many of those years, the Miami Dolphins enjoyed a tremendous home field advantage. Because the heat in Miami, Florida is scorching hot in the months of September and October, the team would enjoy a competitive advantage over many teams.

It was during those years of consistency, which were primarily under legendary head coach, the late great Don Shula, that the Dolphins experienced the most success as a franchise. In 1970, the fortune of the Miami Dolphins organization commenced to improve for the better. The Dolphins suffered through four straight losing seasons from the team's inaugural season in 1966 to 1969 before coach Shula was able to help change the organization's tradition and culture.

No one can talk or reminisce about those years of consistency in winning and success, without mentioning the influence of coach Shula on the Miami Dolphins. Although, I have never had the pleasure of personally meeting the late legendary coach, I have heard stories about how demanding he was of himself, his players, as well as the assistant coaches on his coaching staff that coached under him. Coach Shula set the standard for the winning tradition the Miami Dolphins would enjoy for three glorious decades.

In the American Football Conference, the Miami Dolphins were generally the conference's golden standard primarily during the franchise's approximately quarter of a century success. The National Football League has always been a league comprised of exceptional football players and athletes. When it comes to the success of a team, talent alone is not the only determining factor that will ensure a team's tradition of winning.

There are other variables, which could influence a team's success in the National Football League. For example, players and coaches who are exceptional leaders will hold each member of the team accountable for their play. Also, a talented front office and talent scouts must be in place in order to pick the players from the college draft, who is the right fit for their respective teams.

Hall of Fame general manager, Bobby Beathard was player personnel director for the Miami Dolphins from 1972-1977. His talent at finding players with sensational ability helped position the Dolphins as one of the elite franchises during his tenure. Identifying a player's talent and character is just as vital to a team's success, as an all-world player or coach.

Though, the coaching/general manager tandem of Shula and Beathard helped mold the Miami Dolphins into a perennial playoff contender, the offensive and defensive assistants also influenced the team's culture of winning. Coach Howard Schnellenberger, who is best known for coaching the University of Miami's first college football championship, and innovative defensive guru, coach Bill Arnsparger, who was the architect of the "No Name Defense" were also instrumental in the years of consistency.

Due to the competitive nature of the N.F.L., it is always difficult for any team to remain "top dog." When an organization is known for winning, there are other organizations that are "chomping at the bit" to take that organization's place as a winner. The Dolphins franchise is known for their undefeated and Super Bowl winning season of 1972.

The following year, in 1973, the Dolphins did not end the season with an undefeated record, but statistically the team was better than ever. Also, I would be remiss if I did not mention the Dolphins' 1971 team. That team made it to the Super Bowl in only coach Shula's second season at the helm.

For three consecutive years, the Miami Dolphins were the only team to experience three straight years in the ultimate game, the Super Bowl. This distinction was enjoyed by the Dolphins' franchise, until the divisional rival, Buffalo Bills teams made it to four consecutive Super Bowls in the 1990s. During those years of consistency for the Miami Dolphins, no team dominated one opponent like the Miami Dolphins dominated the Buffalo Bills of the 1970s.

Though, the streak is not the most consecutive wins in N.F.L. history, with the longest streak being held by the Washington Redskins over the Detroit Lions (21 consecutive wins from 1939-2013), these teams are not divisional opponents. As for the Miami Dolphins dominance over the divisional rival Bills, the team could always pencil in a win twice a year for an entire decade (1970-1980). This consecutive win total is so impressive for three reasons.

The first reason why the Dolphins' consecutive game win total over the Buffalo Bills was extremely remarkable is because the Dolphins beat the Bills in their home stadium, as well as the opponent's home turf. This is a difficult accomplishment to achieve, due to the hostile environment and home-field advantage of any particular professional football team. Every team in the N.F.L., that is the home team has the psychological advantage of being in the friendly confines of home, as well as also being in familiar territory.

Another reason why the Dolphins' dominance over the Bills in the decade of the 1970s was extraordinary is the extreme weather in both cities. Miami, Florida is known for its tropical climate basically all year long. Buffalo, New York, on the other hand, is known for its frigid temperatures and swirling winds in the winter months. To win consecutive away games for a team that plays their games in the warm climate of Southern Florida, over a team and city, which is known for its cold weather is nothing short of extremely fortunate and amazing.

Lastly, another reason why the Dolphins' consecutive win streak over the divisional rival, Buffalo Bills was both amazing and shocking is due to the talented play of Hall of Fame Buffalo Bills running back, O.J. Simpson. Simpson was best known for his electric long touchdown runs and also accomplishing the first 2000-yard rushing season in N.F.L. history. The decade long dominance that the Miami Dolphins experienced and achieved over the Buffalo Bills was the epitome of what consistency looks like on the field.

Fortunately for the Miami Dolphins franchise, the organization had the fortune of drafting two Hall of Fame quarterbacks who contributed to the team's success. Quarterback Bob Griese was the Super Bowl winning quarterback who helped bring two world championships to the city of Miami after the 1972 and 1973 seasons. Although, the quarterback did not win another Super Bowl since the 1973 season, he still has the distinction of being the only Dolphins' quarterback to play in three consecutive Super Bowls.

Griese was the starting quarterback for the Miami Dolphins for 14 glorious seasons. Statistically, he might not be the franchise's all-time leader in passing statistics, but the quarterback was truly a winner. During the years that Griese played, the Dolphins had only one losing season. Also, the team did not finish a season during his time at quarterback lower than third place out of five teams within the division. Griese made the pro bowl six times.

In 1977, Griese was the N.F.L. leader in touchdown passes with 22. There is also something else that the former Dolphin quarterback would become known for. It was an object that many of us have in our possession.

The object that I am referring to is glasses. Before Hall of Fame basketball star, Kareem Abdul Jabbar and Hall of Fame running back, Eric Dickerson made wearing goggles famous and en vogue, Griese was the originator in having eye wear worn during a game. After his retirement in 1980, the Dolphins tradition of drafting a Hall of Fame quarterback continued, which contributed to the franchise's consistent tradition of winning football games.

Quarterback, Dan Marino succeeded Bob Griese three years after the Dolphin great called it a career. As I previously stated, Marino was not fortunate enough to win a Super Bowl, but when he played, there was always excitement that filled the stadium in Miami. During Marino's storied career, which he all played with the Miami Dolphins, he would also share in that distinction with his predecessor, Bob Griese.

Under Marino's direction, the Dolphins were usually in the thick of the playoff chase. He was the undisputed face of the organization, which benefited from his leadership and his ability to will the Dolphins to victory. I still can recall those autumn days in sunny Miami when the Dolphins were behind in the fourth quarter.

It seemed that Marino's right arm would determine the outcome of many of the Dolphins' games in the 1980s and 1990s. Like his predecessor, Marino only suffered one losing season while he was the signal caller for the team. Watching Marino and the Dolphins during his time with the team was a joy to watch as a fan.

With many of the games while Marino was at the helm at quarterback, I do not recall a plethora of lop-sided losses. Most fans during his era were assured of two things. For starters, Dolphins fans during Marino's tenure with the team knew that they would generally be in striking distance of winning just about every game that he suited up for. Also, while he played, most fans could enjoy the excitement of his long touchdown passes and game winning drives.

Most teams that are successful in the N.F.L. for a substantial amount of time typically play with intelligence and within the rules. The Dolphins were one of the few teams who would become known for playing a fair game. Unlike some teams, that were known for bending the rules from time to time, or committing errors on the field that would either stop a touchdown drive or hurt the team by accumulating a plethora of penalty yards, the Miami Dolphins were fortunate during the Don Shula era of being a team that the opposing team would have to beat "fair and square."

One of the reasons for the Dolphins' success under the Shula regime was the fact that the Dolphins typically played smart football. And who could blame the Dolphins for being a fundamentally sound football team. Coach Shula was a prominent member of the National Football League's competition and rules committee. He would be one of the committee's members for several years.

It was beneficial to the Miami Dolphins' success because it helped the team as a whole to have full knowledge of the dos and don'ts of what each individual at their respective positions could do on the field. From 1973 to 1987, the Miami

Dolphins enjoyed the distinction of being one of the N.F.L.'s least penalized teams. There is a plethora of preparation that a football team must consider when trying to play the game in the right way.

A team could have all the talent in the world, but if the team is always committing some kind of error, then the team's talent will not become much of a factor. I believe that a team who is penalized the most will typically lack discipline. No team or individual who desires to become one of the league's elite can play the game with reckless abandon because it always affects the whole entire team in the end.

Football is not only a team sport. It is also a performance and results sport. When a team commits a plethora of penalties, typically, the team's performance is bad. Penalties on the field are football's version of rules and mistakes.

I compare penalties on the field with someone who is taking a test. Many of us understand what it is like to go over an assignment for test taking. Each individual player in the N.F.L. must become well-rehearsed each week on what does or does not constitute a penalty on the field.

Once a player is aware of what is deemed a penalty by the N.F.L. officials and referees, then he can rely upon what he studied in the playbook for the weekly opponent. The goal for every football team should be to play the game within the rules, without thinking too much about what to do. This is why preparation is so imperative.

Although, penalties on the field are inevitable, because no team can go through a whole game, let alone, a season without committing some type of penalty, the team that wins the penalty battle will usually put themselves in a position to win. Becoming a team that commits the least amount of penalties requires cohesiveness amongst the 22 players on each side of the ball. The Miami Dolphins proved their cohesiveness and discipline by being one of the most consistent teams in winning, during the first 30 years of the franchise's existence.

Successful football franchises do not necessarily have to win the Super Bowl every year. In the National Football League, it is almost impossible to maintain that high level of consistency. When a football franchise is fortunate enough to have success for a substantial amount of time, in many cases the organization's success could be challenged and threatened.

Before the onset of free agency in 1992, most teams were able to sustain their talent level. Prior to that season, most fans could gain familiarity with the players on the roster of their favorite football team. It was during that era before free agency and player movement commenced when the Miami Dolphins enjoyed their most success as an organization.

When the A.F.L. (American Football League) merged with the N.F.L. (National Football League) in 1970, the Miami Dolphins were one of the teams from the American Football League that would experience success when the teams in that league transitioned into a permanent mainstay in the N.F.L. The original A.F.L. teams, the Dallas Texans who would later become the Kansas City Chiefs, the former and now defunct, Houston Oilers, the original Los Angeles Chargers, who would spend many seasons in San Diego, the Buffalo Bills, the New York Titans, who would later be called the Jets, the Denver Broncos, the Oakland Raiders, and rounding out the former American Football League was the Boston Patriots, who are now known as the New England Patriots, also made the transition into the more conservative National Football League, along with the Miami Dolphins, which formed in 1966, who were members of the American Football League, but not one of the original teams in that league, which formed in 1960.

The Dolphins' franchise became successful in 1970 after joining the A.F.L. in 1966. Former American Football League teams like the Kansas City Chiefs and the Oakland Raiders also became prominent teams of success after the A.F.L./ N.F.L. merger. From 1970 to 2001, the Dolphins played in 22 postseason games during that 32- year period. Of 528 possible games, the Miami Dolphins would win 273 of those games, while only having 2 ties.

This equated to an overall winning percentage of 63.6. Having a high winning percentage for a team that only came into existence in 1966 is extremely extraordinary. Winning in the National Football League requires commitment, passion, as well as dedication.

During those seasons of perennial playoff contention, winning for the Dolphins' franchise was highly anticipated and expected. Though, the Miami Dolphins typically appeared in white uniforms, due to the extreme heat in South Florida, it was during those years of success for those Dolphin teams that every team who played the Dolphins would not consider the team as a "pushover" or "doormat." Some considered teams who wore white in the rugged game of football as inferior. Dolphin teams during those first 32 years after the merger were typically tough and intelligent.

Monday Night Football became a football phenomenon in the 1970s and 1980s. It is still a primetime game that currently consists of teams in the N.F.L. who are typically good and dominant. The individuals who made up the schedule for the teams to appear in the primetime game would not waste the television viewer's time by scheduling inferior teams in Mondays' football showdown.

Because the Miami Dolphins were a winning and successful football franchise consistently for many seasons, the schedule makers ultimately rewarded the franchise's success by having the team appear in that game regularly. The Dolphins would hold the distinction of being the only team in the entire league to appear in the Monday Night game the most times. The game is rewarded to teams who are successful by N.F.L. standards and that says a lot for a team, especially, the Miami Dolphins.

At the time that I am writing this book, the Miami Dolphins have appeared in the primetime Monday Night football game a whopping 87 times. Some might suggest that successful teams such as, the Dallas Cowboys, Pittsburgh Steelers, San Francisco 49ers, or New England Patriots would have appeared more times than the Miami Dolphins, but this is a record and title that would be the Dolphins franchise's own. In my opinion, being the team with the most Monday night appearances demonstrates the team's winning tradition and excellence.

This particular game is viewed every Monday night during the football season by millions of football fans nationwide. Many of the other N.F.L. franchises and teams who are competing in the league would love to become featured on the Monday night platform. Appearing in that game basically conveys a message to the other N.F.L. teams and personnel around the league that a team's appearance means that the team was successful in the previous season.

If a team made the playoffs in the previous season, then the team could almost for certain make a Monday night appearance. Unfortunately, though the Dolphins have the most appearances in the primetime game, they do not have the most victories. As a fan, I would like them to also share that distinction with the Pittsburgh Steelers, who have the distinction of enjoying the most victories with 56 wins, at the time of the writing of this book, but the Dolphins are still amongst the all-time Monday night victories list with 43 wins, which places them at fifth all-time.

Exposure is what any team can gain from appearing on Monday Night Football. The Miami Dolphins have enjoyed many years of nationwide exposure with their consistent play between 1970-2001. Some have been able to become fans of the team without having to set foot on Miami soil.

Due to consistency in winning, the Dolphins were able to enjoy being one of the elite N.F.L. teams who were in the national spotlight for many years. Playing on Monday night has afforded the Miami Dolphins franchise fans in places that the players and organization as a whole could not have imagined. A winning product on the field will always attract new fans nationwide, and perhaps worldwide.

Making it to the Super Bowl is difficult for every team. Most teams are not assured of ever playing in the big game. In the 1970s and 1980s, no team can claim more appearances in the Super Bowl than the Miami Dolphins.

Many fans around the N.F.L. do not know that known fact. The Dolphins were fortunate enough to make the Super Bowl five times. Their first Super Bowl appearance was against the Dallas Cowboys after the 1971 season. It resulted in an unforgettable loss for the Shula lead Dolphins, which fueled the team's dominance for the next two Super Bowls.

Of course, most N.F.L. fans are aware of the 1972 season, which was the magical undefeated season that ended in a perfect 14-0 record. The Dolphins defeated the Washington Redskins in the Coliseum Stadium in Los Angeles, California. Though, I was born during the next Super Bowl winning season in 1973, I have seen the highlights of the 1972 Super Bowl win.

In that 1972 Super Bowl, it was a game that was dominated by the Dolphins. 1973 would also be the year of the Miami Dolphins when they manhandled the N.F.C. Conference Champion, Minnesota Vikings at Rice Stadium in Houston, Texas, winning by the score of 24-7. Unfortunately, for the Miami Dolphins, 1973 would become the last season the franchise would have the fortune of hoisting a Super Bowl trophy.

From 1974 until the strike-shortened season of 1982, the Dolphins would still participate in the playoffs four times during that span. 1982 would be the year that the Miami Dolphins would return to the ultimate game. After approximately a ten-year hiatus from the World Championship of the N.F.L., the Dolphins would face a familiar foe in the John Riggins lead Washington Redskins in Super Bowl XVII.

I do recall viewing this game as a 9- year old youngster. The game ended in dramatic fashion with the Redskins' Riggins breaking the arm tackle of Dolphins' cornerback, Don McNeal late in the fourth quarter. This game played in January of 1983 would ultimately become the closest the Miami Dolphins would come to winning a Super Bowl title since 1973.

Super Bowl XIX, the game that I previously discussed, marked the 5th and final appearance in the Super Bowl for the A.F.C. East's, Miami Dolphins. I remember how often the Dolphins would make the playoffs between 1981-1985. Those Shula lead teams of the 1970s and 1980s really had a winning edge.

Until the Pittsburgh Steelers and San Francisco 49ers dynasties of the 1970s and 1980s, no other N.F.L. franchise could claim to be a participant of more than four Super Bowl games. A team that makes it to the Super Bowl will typically have a difficult time in the following season. That team will have a target on them when teams play them.

Now the Dolphins were not winning multiple Super Bowls after the 1972-73 seasons, but during the decades of the 1970s and 1980s, it was common for the Miami Dolphins to be mentioned amongst Super Bowl contenders. Winning a Super Bowl is no small feat. But getting to the "big game" is a feat that both teams appearing in the Super Bowl within any given year cannot ignore.

Losing for the Miami Dolphins between 1970-2003 was never commonplace. In those 33 seasons, the Dolphins franchise only experienced two losing seasons. If that does not epitomize consistency, then I do not know what else will.

Winning in the National Football League for many of the league's teams is filled with many peaks and valleys. Most teams have a window of opportunity when it comes to winning. Injuries could plague a franchise, or the stars of the team could either retire or be traded to another organization.

Though, the Dolphins organization cannot boast about winning a plethora of Super Bowls, the Dolphin teams that were generally on the field, typically, played a winning brand of football. Year in and year out, many of the sports commentators would always factor in the Dolphins as a team that was always aspiring to win. With the distractions of South Beach, winning for the Dolphins during those 33 years of consistency should be viewed as more than just a casual accomplishment.

Winning for all of those years is downright impressive. Think about the teams that have won consistently in the N.F.L. recently. They were not always dominant. A team like the Pittsburgh Steelers was commonly referred to as the team of the 1970s.

Many young fans of that era do not know how that team and organization experienced many decades of losing prior to their own winning tradition. There are also other teams in the N.F.L. who are currently known as a winning franchise and organization, but they too experienced many lean years before the team was able to break away from its losing pattern. The San Francisco 49ers, known as the team of the 1980s, also did not enjoy years of consistency in winning prior to winning multiple Super Bowls.

The Miami Dolphins franchise is still relatively young. Currently, it has only existed for 58 years. There are some parents, and grandparents who are considerably older than the

Dolphins franchise its self. Fortunately, the Miami Dolphins were able to win with consistency early and often.

It is due to the organization's early success that winning for the Miami Dolphins became a normal tradition and process. Briefly, I stated that playing in South Florida could become an unwanted distraction. The city of Miami is well known for its clubs and nightlife.

Focusing on football and winning with consistency could become difficult to accomplish when a jet setting lifestyle is competing for a young player's attention. In the late 1970s and early 1980s, the city of Miami became known for drugs and violence. Individuals living in that culture and society during that time had a safe haven on Sundays when the Dolphins were playing and winning almost 64% of the time.

Growing up in the 1980s, the Miami Dolphins organization was to me a world-class franchise. The product on the field, which featured many talented players, was undeniable. Whether the Dolphins won or lost, I knew that fans during that era would always receive their money's worth when watching them.

Don Shula's 26 years and 274 victories including playoff victories with the Miami Dolphins, contributed to the organization's consistency of success. When Shula retired after the 1995 season, I had an inkling that the trajectory of the franchise would ultimately change. The day that Shula was no longer the Miami Dolphins' head coach, was the day that I knew the Miami Dolphins would not be the same franchise.

On January 4th 1996, which was Coach Shula's birthday, I immediately knew that the Dolphins' years of consistency would no longer be a reality., I can remember how I felt when the mainstay of the Miami Dolphins organization participated in his "going away party." I must admit that I cried like a baby on that day. The Dolphins' organization during that time did not understand how Shula's eventual retirement would have a significant impact.

Now I do not believe that coach Shula is the only reason why the Miami Dolphins enjoyed many seasons of consistency and success, but I believe that the late great legendary coach played a vital role in the franchise's consistency. During the Miami Dolphins' reign of consistency, I never imagined that it would one day cease. But in life, especially, in the game of football, nothing remains forever.

The game of professional football is a business. Sometimes in business, the owner or CEO of a franchise would like to experience the next big thing. Dolphin fans have not had the luxury of enjoying the next big thing in recent years after Hall of Fame quarterback, Dan Marino and the late Hall of Fame coach, Don Shula's untimely retirements.

I believe the Dolphins organization, as well as its fans miss those days that the team was mentioned amongst the National Football League's elite teams. Though, in previous years, the franchise has not been able to enjoy consistency in winning, the franchise is still in the top ten of winning organizations in the N.F.L. Sometimes a team or franchise can become complacent when it is experiencing an adequate amount of success.

Teams and also fans whose teams win with consistency could take success for granted. The Dolphins teams between 1970-2003 spoiled its fans in South Florida and all throughout the nation with its winning culture. As a loyal fan, I have also been guilty of having a complacent attitude towards the team.

1992 was the last A.F.C. Championship appearance for the aqua and orange. The team would make the playoffs since that year, but the playoff success when some of the Dolphins teams did make it into the playoff tournament did not result in the same kind of success that the franchise enjoyed in previous years. Nevertheless, the Dolphins still managed to win a few Wild Card playoff games since then.

In the decade of the 1990s, the Dolphins organization would have three coaches in seven years. After coach Shula retired after the 1995 season, the team hired Hall of Fame coach, Jimmy Johnson in 1996 to continue the winning tradition. Though, his stint with the Dolphins did not result in a Super Bowl victory, the team made the playoffs three out of Johnson's four seasons.

After Johnson's abrupt retirement in 2000, following a horrific playoff loss to the Jacksonville Jaguars, coach Dave Wannstedt led the Dolphins to the divisional round of the playoffs in 2000 and 2001. Before his firing during the 2004 regular season, Wannstedt helped the Dolphins finish the previous three seasons with no less than 9 victories in the regular season, while also leading the team to a division title in 2000.

Producing a winning culture and tradition is a difficult and challenging feat. In the N.F.L., having just one winning season is not easy to accomplish, but multiple seasons of winning means that the organization is elite and special. The Miami Dolphins were not just a unique franchise because they are the only N.F.L. franchise in the Super Bowl era to follow an undefeated regular season with a Super Bowl victory.

What made the Dolphins organization a step above many of the other N.F.L. organizations and franchises around the league for decades, was the team's consistency and longevity in having a winning tradition and culture. Some N.F.L. organizations can only dream of having the Dolphins' decades long success. The late owner of the Miami Dolphins, Joe Robbie had a vision for the team when he and his family owned the franchise over those two successful decades.

Under the previous ownership of Mr. Robbie and the Robbie family, the Dolphins were the most consistent. When the Miami

Dolphins were a lowly expansion franchise in the American Football League, the team's mascot, "Flipper the dolphin" was the only constant and main attraction when the Dolphins initially commenced playing their home games in the former Orange Bowl stadium in 1966. Flipper could be viewed in a tank at the back of the end zone, which provided entertainment for the once floundering and struggling franchise, when the live mascot would jump in the tank after every scored touchdown or field goal.

When the Dolphins franchise commenced to win games with more consistency beginning in the 1970 season, winning football games became the source of success, instead of a cute and live mammal that was previously the star of the popular television series that aired on NBC from 1964-1967. The Miami Dolphins created their own version of must-see television with consistency in winning that provided plenty of entertainment for Dolphins fans everywhere. Fans would enjoy a plethora of famed regular season and playoff games, which would serve as pleasant memories of consistency in winning for seasoned Dolphins fans.

Though, the Miami Dolphins have not enjoyed a Super Bowl victory in 50 years, this does not negate the organization's success during those years of regular post-season visits. Nor, does it erase the fact that the Miami Dolphins franchise is one of the National Football League's most storied and popular franchises. A casual fan might not know the rich history of the Miami Dolphins, but if they would ever look up a professional football team that was undefeated, the Dolphins franchise will prominently appear.

The Miami Dolphins era of consistency is gradually returning, but the memories of winning success have provided a blueprint of what longevity in winning looks like. No fan of the team should feel slighted because the franchise does not have more than two world championships. I will always cherish those years of consistency with hopes that the winning culture and elite status will soon return.

CHAPTER 3
The Shula Effect

Pacing the sidelines with his trademark sunglasses and distinctive jaw, coach Don Shula could intimidate many of the referees he came in contact with on the sidelines. I can recall seeing the legendary coach becoming filled with emotion when a call was missed, or when the team was penalized. The first thing that I thought about when I would watch coach Shula on the sidelines was passion.

When an individual is passionate about something that typically means that the individual loves it. In my opinion, the Hall of Fame coach loved the Miami Dolphins. Think about it. In the modern era of football, it was unheard of to coach a professional football team for over ten years, let alone 26 years with the same organization.

Most coaches get burned out from coaching after several years. I believe that coach Shula would have coached the Miami Dolphins well into his 70s if he had remained the coach of the team. Some ignorantly speculated that Shula lost his influence on the team in his last few seasons of coaching

How can someone make that claim? In coach Shula's last five seasons with the Miami Dolphins, the team finished each of those seasons with no less than 8 regular season wins. The Dolphins last appeared in the A.F.C. Championship game in 1992 when Shula was the coach of the team. 1995 was the legendary coach's last full season at the helm, and the Dolphins still managed to make the playoffs under his leadership. Though, his team would lose to the division rival, Buffalo Bills, 37-22, in the Wild Card game, as a fan I did not get the sense that the game was passing Shula by.

This non-factual jargon is what I heard in the years leading up to his retirement. During Shula's era of coaching, he coached against other legendary coaches, like Hall of Fame coach Tom Landry, of the Dallas Cowboys, and Hall of Fame coach of the Pittsburgh Steelers, Chuck Noll. Coach Shula would go on to coach longer than these well-known coaches, while enjoying more coaching success compared to those legendary coaches in their last seasons with their respective teams.

In fact, I can vividly recall how in the last seasons of coaches Tom Landry and Chuck Noll's tenure with their teams how those teams were not as competitive as they were in seasons past. Coach Shula's teams made the playoffs in three of his last five seasons on the sidelines. The other two teams that did not make the playoffs in 1991 and 1993, barely missed making the playoff tournament, which ultimately came down to the last game of those seasons.

As I reflect back to those last five seasons of Shula's coaching career, I can honestly state without bias that the winning culture of the franchise was still intact. If Shula lost his handle over the team, then the product on the field would have been affected by it. Under coach Shula, I do not recall many lop-sided losses, or shutouts during his tenure as the Miami Dolphins head man. No one can claim that coach Shula's teams were not consistently competitive during his watch.

Another man's trash is another man's treasure is an old saying that many have heard in their lifetime. When coach Shula's relationship with former Baltimore Colts owner, the late Carroll Rosenbloom became strained after the Colts' lost to Joe Namath and the New York Jets in Super Bowl III, the Hall of Fame coach became expendable. The late owner did not foresee how the young talented coach would become a "shining star" to a struggling franchise for years to come.

In the N.F.L. patience is typically not a virtue. Most owners, as well as some fans would prefer to win immediately. Thankfully, for the Miami Dolphins when coach Shula arrived, the Dolphins organization did not have to experience a long process of building a winning team. The legendary head coach was forty-years of age when he took over as the Dolphins' coaching leader.

He was young enough to participate in the Miami heat with his players while they were training for the upcoming season in 1970. I can recall viewing Shula working out with the team on old video recordings. There were some players who would faint or pass out due to coach Shula's intense program regimen.

Before Shula's arrival, I can speculate how many of the Dolphins players were content to remain in that same stagnant status of losing football games. Just like winning, losing can also become contagious. If one player on the team is accepting of losing, then it could have both a domino and cancerous effect throughout the rest of the team.

Coach Shula had been known as a young and talented coach prior to his arrival in Miami, but his Colts teams had a plethora of veterans. There was a long running joke when Shula was the coach of the Baltimore Colts that the players were just as old as him. He took over as coach of the veteran Colts at 33 years of age.

Seven years later, Shula had the challenge and task of molding a team of young impressionable players into a team of champions. He also had great power and control over the organization. Shula's powers included general manager type duties, as well as a 10% ownership stake with the Miami Dolphins.

All of those perks could have been detrimental to the coach's quest to change the trajectory of a once struggling expansion American Football League franchise. Most individuals who are given that much control over an organization will neglect other aspects of the franchise, which could also affect the team that essentially lays their bodies on the line each Sunday. After it was deemed that late owner of the Miami Dolphins, Joe Robbie was in violation of the tampering policy by the late N.F.L. commissioner, Pete Rozelle, to get Shula to coach the Dolphins at the beginning of the 1970 season, the only penalty for Robbie and the Dolphins organization during that time was the team's first-round draft pick in 1971, which would be awarded to the Baltimore Colts in exchange for coach Shula's services. In hindsight, when you think about the Baltimore Colts acquiring the Dolphins draft pick for one year, in order to have Shula patrolling the sidelines for 26 wonderful years, I can conclude that the Miami Dolphins truly won the exchange.

If any individual desires to have any type of success in life, that individual must not be fearful of acquiring discipline. Discipline and lack thereof can make a world of difference. In the game of professional football, a disciplined team will be able to enjoy the perks of success in the end.

Briefly, I discussed how Shula's teams were amongst the least penalized teams for a significant portion of his coaching tenure. It is when the team is collectively disciplined that the team could be in a more favorable position to win. Disciplined teams must have commitment and focus.

The Dolphins enjoyed success under coach Shula because of the team's hard-nosed discipline. Offensive lines are typically the closest individuals on each team in football. Skilled players, like wide receivers and running backs, do not have the scrutiny of discipline that individuals who play on the offensive line have.

These big mammoths of human beings are responsible for keeping the quarterback protected, as well as opening up holes for halfbacks and fullbacks trying to vie for yardage. An average fan might not realize how a disciplined offensive line is vital to a team's success. Coach Shula's teams had other units on the team who received national acclaim.

On the defensive side of the ball in the early 1970s, the "No-Name Defense" rose to fame during those Super Bowl years. It received its name by late Dallas Cowboys Hall of Fame coach Tom Landry. That defense was a talented bunch that played with discipline and toughness.

Led by the late Hall of Fame linebacker, Nick Buoniconti, late defensive end, Bill Stanfill, defensive tackle Manny Fernandez, and safeties Dick Anderson and the late Jack Scott, this unit, like its offensive were a force to become wrecked with. In the early 1980s, a disciplined defense under head coach, Don Shula would also become thrust into national prominence. I am referring to the defensive unit, affectionately known as, the "Killer Bees."

The Killer Bees were comprised of defensive tackles Bob Baumhower, and Doug Betters, defensive end, Kim Bokamper, linebackers, Charles Bowser and Bob Brudzinki, and brothers, Lyle and Glenn Blackwood, who were defensive backs. Though, the defensive units I just stated were extremely vital in Shula's disciplined teams, the offensive line units were also a main reason why Dolphins teams during Shula's era could receive the distinction of being disciplined. There were talented Hall of Fame, offensive lineman, who played for the Miami Dolphins under former head coach, Don Shula, who demonstrated the toughness and discipline that a Don Shula coached team, would become known for. These men are offensive lineman, Jim Langer, the late Bob Kuechenburg, Larry Little, and center Dwight Stephenson.

Miami, Florida was known as a sleepy beach town upon Don Shula's arrival. It was a town that was a desired location for individuals who were ready to retire and settle in a beach community. When coach Shula helped turn the Dolphins franchise into a perennial winner, the town began to blossom from a town of retirees to a town of movers and shakers.

Shula's imprint on the South Florida metropolitan area still looms large. Due to his years of consistency in winning, as well as lending his name to charitable causes throughout the area, the legendary coach, though, not a native of the city of Miami was adopted into the region, as Southern Florida's own. Coach Shula was not just a successful football coach and N.F.L. icon.

He was also a businessman and product influencer. Shula's steakhouses, bars, and grills would become a permanent fixture in the state of Florida and elsewhere. As a product influencer, he helped advertise such companies as NutriSystem diet plans, Humana health insurance, as well as having the distinction of becoming the first American to sign up for Medicare Part D prescription drug plan benefits. Coach Shula's name will always be embedded in the city of Miami.

The legendary coach had hotels, streets, and causeways named after him. If people in the general area where an individual made his or her living for over a quarter of a century would like to honor that individual with naming something in that town or area after that individual, then I can assure you that the individual did something right. Winning football games with consistency helped coach Shula and the city of Miami gain national awareness and prominence.

Although, his accomplishments are stellar on the field, he might not have known how his will to win within the rules helped a young black kid who grew up in Texas how to strive for perfection. I noticed how Shula was demanding of his players when I would view him in various games, but I also knew that he always wanted what was best for his team and organization. Some view a relationship between a coach and a franchise in the same way that one might view a marriage.

In these modern times, it is unlikely that a marriage will last until "death do you part." The game of professional football could be viewed in that same sense because when a coach is hired, he is obligated to that franchise or organization for the time being. Either the organization can honor the coach by giving him an extension on his contract, which will give him more incentive to remain with the organization, or one or both of the parties involved could mutually agree to part ways.

When it comes to the football marriage between coach Shula and the Miami Dolphins it was a long and prosperous one. Did it have difficult and hard times? Of course there were challenges and adversities that coach Shula experienced while coaching the team. Though, times were not always ideal between the legendary coach and the organization, Shula still epitomized loyalty to the city of Miami, as well as the Miami Dolphins organization.

Change could become a threat for anyone. Coaches, especially, those who are in the N.F.L. have philosophical styles when it comes to their team's identity. In many instances, a N.F.L. head coach will not deviate from his philosophical vision for the team.

Many coaches are stubborn when it comes to the style of play that they would prefer. For example, the late legendary and Hall of Fame Green Bay Packers and Washington Redskins coach, Vince Lombardi's philosophical vision was having a sound running game. Throughout his entire career, Lombardi won many games with that offensive approach.

Coach Shula, on the other hand, was not as rigid as other N.F.L. head coaches who coached during his era, in regard to adopting a new or different kind of offensive approach in winning football games. There are some coaches who are currently coaching who will not change with the times. Shula, began his illustrious coaching career by coaching the late great quarterback, Johnny Unitas, Hall of Fame receiver, Raymond Berry and talented pass catcher, the late Jimmy Orr, the late great innovative tight end, Hall of Fame inductee, John Mackey, as well as Hall of Fame running and pass receiving threat, Lenny Moore.

The offense during Shula's tenure with the Baltimore Colts was primarily a balanced offense with the potential of scoring touchdowns by either running the football, or passing the football downfield on long touchdown scoring passes. Once Shula settled in Miami in 1970, he did have a talented receiving threat in former Cleveland Browns and Miami Dolphins Hall of Fame wide receiver, Paul Warfield, but ultimately the philosophical approach that Shula chose to adopt in the early 1970s was primarily the run-first mentality of the old National Football League. In the early 1980s, Shula switched his offensive philosophical style to primarily a pass-first oriented offense.

This brand of offense became the permanent fixture in Shula's offensive philosophy throughout the 1980s and mid-1990s, until his retirement in 1995. Coach Shula proved that he was not "stuck in his ways." He could adapt his vision and philosophical approach to his offensive talent and strengths.

When quarterback Bob Griese played up until the 1980 season, the offensive playing styles of many teams around the N.F.L. were more safe and conservative. An offense that is predicated on the running game was typically safe and predictable. In the 1983 season, which was Hall of Fame quarterback, Dan Marino's rookie season with the Miami Dolphins, head coach, Don Shula decided to change and adapt his offensive approach and philosophy to give what he thought would become the team's best chance to win with regularity.

A pass- first offensive philosophy was exciting for many Dolphins fans around the country, but Shula's changed philosophical approach never again netted him another Super Bowl ring or trophy. It was commendable for Shula to change with a more open offensive philosophy, but having a one-dimensional offense would also become a curse by putting a plethora of pressure on Dan Marino and his talented receiving core, as well as on the defense due to the offense's quick strike capabilities. If the Shula/Marino era had a sound running game, I would be curious to know if their careers would have become even more successful than it already was.

Delegating the coaching responsibilities and duties served well under coach Shula. It is almost impossible to enjoy an extreme amount of coaching success without competent assistant coaches. Though, Shula is given much of the credit for turning the Dolphins franchise into instant winners, his assistant coaches were very much involved with the success of the Miami Dolphins.

In my opinion, an N.F.L. head coach is just as good as his loyal assistants. Due to the tireless efforts and sacrifices of N.F.L. assistants, a team is in a position to win on Sundays. What I admired most about coach Shula was the fact that he did not publicly have an air of arrogance when he was interviewed either after a hard-fought win or a devastating loss.

Also, when the Dolphins lost, he did not utter out any excuses. Typically, Shula won or lost with his team of well-qualified and loyal assistant coaches. There are two assistant coaches, who coached under coach Shula, that do not receive a ton of credit for their contributions to coach Shula's success.

The late defensive line coach Mike (Mo) Scarry, was instrumental to both of the Miami Dolphins prominent defensive units, the "No-Name Defense" in the early 1970s, as well as the "Killer Bee Defense" of the early 1980s. Scarry worked closely with defensive guru, the late great

Bill Arnsparger, who as I previously stated, was the primary architect of both of those innovative defensive teams. Scarry spent 16 years as defensive line coach, and later run defense coordinator, until he retired after the 1985 season.

Ironically, the Dolphins never played in another Super Bowl, since Scarry's departure from the Dolphins. Another coach, who definitely deserves credit for coach Shula's effect and success with the Miami Dolphins, is longtime assistant and offensive line coach, John Sandusky. He joined the Dolphins in 1976, and remained the offensive line coach under coach Shula for 19 seasons, until his retirement in 1994.

Under Sandusky's tutelage, the offensive line play was superb, and considered one of the best offensive line units in the N.F.L. during his time as the Dolphins' offensive line coach. Because the offensive line play continued to be amongst the elite in the N.F.L., the Dolphins offensive line did not have the unwanted distinction of leading the league in allowing the most sacks, hits, and quarterback pressures on the quarterback. In addition, Sandusky's offensive line units were disciplined and did not commit a plethora of penalties and mental errors.

Coach Shula has reportedly said," I've been blessed with some great assistant coaches." Shula said this quote in a 2012 interview with the Fort Myers News-Press, in regard to the passing of former defensive line coach and run defense coordinator, "Mo Scarry." Coaches, players, and other individuals who are fortunate enough to either currently have, or have had employment in the N.F.L. at some point, are guilty of not giving credit to others who have helped them along the way, when it is in that individual's best interest to give someone else praise for having such a profound impact in the life and success of that person. These two coaches with whom I just discussed might not have taken the N.F.L. by storm, but I am certain that coach Shula never forgot how imperative these unsung coaches became vital to his successful winning formula.

Every team in the N.F.L. has a game plan. Game plans are implemented each week by the offensive and defensive coordinators. These specific plans consist of plays and strategies to help the team win the game.

Some coaches swear by the team's strategic plan to attack the opposing opponent. What I mean by a coach who swears by the team's game plan is that the coach will not deviate from the plan no matter what. Sometimes, sticking with the game plan works, and then in other times it can become a hindrance.

Offensive and defensive game plans come into fruition with continuous film study on the team's weekly opponent. Many of the assistant coaches spend long hours at the team's facility in hopes that the strategic plan to become victorious will succeed. What does a team do when the game plan is not working by halftime of the game? Does the team carry on with the game plan grudgingly and stubbornly? Today, most teams make what is now called halftime adjustments in order to have the chance to win the game in the second half of the contest.

Coach Shula was innovative when it came to either changing the game plan, or making adjustments at halftime. In the game of football, adjustments are necessary. There are always peaks and valleys in each game.

What might have worked the last time both teams played could result in the opposing team having the answer to combat it. Halftime adjustments have really helped Shula win a plethora of football games during his time with the Dolphins. For some, who have played or coached under coach Shula, as well as other opposing coaches and players, many would agree that Shula was one of the masters of the halftime adjustment.

When I think of coaches who are stubborn when it comes to game plans and halftime adjustments, immediately closed-mindedness comes to mind. Successful people are always open to new ideas. In professional football, a player or a coach might have noticed a tendency or something that the opposing team might be doing differently, in which the team was not prepared for.

This is the main reason why halftime adjustments are vital and crucial. A football game is not won in the first and second quarter. Though, the last quarter of a football contest is the most significant, the third quarter, after making the necessary adjustments at halftime sets the tone for the rest of the game.

Shula and the Dolphins won a plethora of games by making halftime adjustments. Communication and openness are key factors that a team must have to become amongst the elite teams that are able to win games after having a first half deficit. Coach Shula always had the mindset that a game plan could always be tweaked.

Due to coach Shula's innovative plan to not always stick with the game plan, he and the Dolphins were able to win many of their games in the second half. It requires trust and communication amongst the team at halftime to have the willingness to make adjustments to win games. Now, in the modern N.F.L., half-time adjustments are common, thanks to the openness of coach Shula to not remain stagnant in regard to the game plan.

Integrity is a quality and trait that few have in these modern times. In regard to sports, many players, coaches, and organizations will try to gain a winning edge. While striving for an edge, some will cheat their way to glory.

Don Shula was passionate and emotional when it came to coaching the Miami Dolphins on the sidelines. His teams were generally prepared to battle on the gridiron. Though, Shula's Dolphins were successful while he was the team's coaching leader, they also won with integrity and class. When it comes to a coach and his team, many of the players and assistant coaches are in many cases the reflection of the head coach. There are various types of leaders. Some lead with dishonesty and surliness, while others win with respect and dignity.

Whether coach Shula won or lost, I always saw him with a consistent demeanor. Now I am not saying that he never displayed emotion after a big win because he would sometimes smile. What I mean by Shula's consistent demeanor is that he never belittled the opposing team, or tried to make the team or the opposing coach feel inferior.

During the time that Shula was the Dolphins head coach, I never heard of him or any of his coaches becoming involved in any kind of cheating scandal. As sure as clouds and stars are in the sky each day, Shula's leadership of integrity was always undeniable and consistent. I believe that his faith played a vital role in regard to how he strived to win with honesty and integrity.

Shula's integrity and honesty was in full display in a game against the Oakland Raiders. According to the Hall of Fame fullback, Dolphins great, Larry Csonka, Shula had a golden opportunity to become dishonest, and like many other individuals who are in positions of leadership. Csonka stated in a documentary about the late legendary coach that the game plan for the Raiders was in full view for anyone to see how the team would strategize against them.

Somehow the game plan was in Csonka's possession because according to the great fullback, he saw the Raider's game plan just lying around. Csonka did not know what to do, so he told coach Shula what he had found. Most coaches or average individuals in Shula's position would jump at the chance to have the opponent's game plan at their disposal. The reaction that Shula gave to Csonka was priceless. Because the coach did not want to compromise his integrity, Shula simply told his star fullback to "put the game plan in the trash."

This exchange between the illustrious coach and his talented player could have helped the Dolphins chances of winning an all- important game. Could the abandoned game plan increase the coach's chances of gaining another win under his belt? I would probably say "perhaps." But in typical Shula style, the coach who would later become the National Football League's all-time leader in coaching wins, chose to take "the high road", and maintain his high moral character.

For decades in the N.F.L., white players dominated the offensive line and punting positions. Coach Shula and the Miami Dolphins offensive line coach, John Sandusky were instrumental in giving a young, black, and talented lineman, Dwight Stevenson, a chance to shine on the Dolphins' solid offensive line in the decade of the 1980s. Successful black offensive lineman was unheard of in the preceding seasons before Stevenson would anchor that unit.

Many of the N.F.L. personnel before the 1970s did not view blacks as having the right intelligence and mental makeup to become a successful offensive lineman. Though, there were other black offensive lineman who played considerably well, such as, Oakland Raiders Hall of Fame offensive lineman, the late great, Gene Upshaw, and Art Shell, as well as fellow former Miami Dolphin and Hall of Fame guard, Larry Little, black offensive lineman were typically scarce compared to their white counterparts. Coach Shula did not question center Dwight Stephenson's intelligence.

When Shula and the coaching staff settled on Stephenson as their starting center late in the 1981 season after an injury to the incumbent starting center, Stephenson and the other offensive lineman on the Miami Dolphins emerged as one of the National Football League's best and talented offensive lines. Shula gave the lineman (center Dwight Stephenson) the opportunity to become offensive captain after his consistent and stellar play. Hall of Fame and former Miami Dolphins center Dwight Stephenson is considered one of the best centers to have ever played in the N.F.L.

I believe that inserting Dwight Stevenson into one of the most important positions speaks volumes about coach Shula's mindset. He did not care about Stevenson's complexion. Shula just wanted to put the best player on the field.

The decision to put Stevenson at center truly helped Shula's career to continue to remain on the winning trajectory. Stevenson's talent help propel Shula and the Dolphins into three A.F.C. Championship appearances and two Super Bowls (Super Bowl XVII and Super Bowl XIX). As for the other position in the N.F.L. that few black players have become successful at playing is the punter position.

Though, the late punter, Reggie Roby was not the first black punter in the N.F.L., he still was one of the few black punters who has ever worn an N.F.L. uniform. In the 6th round of the 1983 draft, Shula and the Dolphins drafted the talented and innovative punter. Roby would play ten stellar seasons with the Miami Dolphins. The thing that stands out in regard to Roby is the fact that he would wear a watch on his wrist when he punted the football in order to gauge his hang time. Also, I had never seen a punter that was built like him. Most punters and kickers are typically slight of build. Roby was 6'4 and 250 pounds.

In the 1980s, Shula and the Dolphins' brass drafted two solid players at their respective positions, that played positions, typically, not played by black men. One was a future Hall of Fame inductee, while the other was a solid performer. During the decade of the 1980s, coach Shula proved that he was ahead of his time by having both a black center and punter prominently playing on his team when it was not vogue to have blacks starting in positions that many who are non-black have starred in the past and dominated.

Since coach Shula's departure from the Miami Dolphins, the team has had 11 head coaches, which also includes interim head coaches. My hypothesis was proved correct when I stated to all who would listen that the team would not be the same without him. Shula retired over a quarter of a century ago, and he still remains the golden standard of success and longevity for the Dolphins organization, as well throughout the entire N.F.L.

There are many successful N.F.L. franchises and dynasties that have experienced a plethora of success in the league, but they cannot claim to have a former Hall of Fame coach who demonstrated both integrity and class while winning on a regular basis. Sometimes, some individuals who have enjoyed success and fame cannot live up to their renowned status. In my opinion, coach Shula, though I never met him in this life, seemed as though he did not live in false pretenses. The same individual who coached the Miami Dolphins for 26 glorious seasons is the same individual who was also beloved by former players, coaches, as well as family members.

Many who are in N.F.L. circles cannot mention the Miami Dolphins organization from the 1970s until the mid-1990s without mentioning coach Shula's name. The legendary coach transitioned from this life in May of 2020, but he will always be remembered for being the undisputed coaching mainstay of many competitive teams during his coaching tenure with the franchise. Shula was a famed coach, who also was devout in his faith, which was unheard of for individuals with his magnitude of success.

It was Shula who had various unforgettable quotes that loomed bigger than the game of football. One of his famous quotes that I really enjoy is "Success is not forever, and failure is not fatal." This particular quote epitomizes what life is all about.

Success, like money can be fleeting. In other words, it comes and goes. No one can live in the midst of success in life, every single day of one's life, and when someone does fail in life, it will not kill the individual. What I gather from the last half of that quote is another famous saying" What does not kill you makes you stronger."

Another famous quote from the former legendary Miami Dolphins head coach is " Lead, follow, or get the hell out of the way." This particular quote speaks for its self. Leaders cannot be stopped, so if you cannot lead, then become a follower, but get out of the way if you cannot be a leader or a follower. An individual is either one or the other, and there is not indecisiveness or middle ground in regard to being a leader or a follower, is what I gather from this profound quote.

Shula patrolled the Miami Dolphins sidelines with heart and passion that only a few coaches could ever match, especially, during his coaching prime. His vision of turning the Dolphins franchise into Super Bowl contenders and winners was definitely accomplished. As a loyal and life-long fan of the Miami Dolphins, I would not enjoy approximately 40 seasons of watching Dolphins games without paying homage to the coach, who gave a significant portion of his life to coach the team that would leave an indelible print in my life. The Miami Dolphins would not have its rich culture, history, and winning tradition without coach Don Shula's commitment to passion and discipline.

CHAPTER 4
Heartbreaking Losses

Considered one of the best playoff games ever, the 1974 playoff game between the reigning Super Bowl champions, Miami Dolphins versus the Oakland Raiders was an instant classic. The game was played in Oakland, California and commenced with an 89-yard opening kickoff return by rookie and long-time Dolphin wide receiver, Nat Moore. His touchdown return put the defending champions on top, 7-0.

This was the only score that either team would produce in the whole entire first quarter. Both teams exhibited and played inspired defense. Miami's defense held the passing attack of the Oakland Raiders in check.

It seemed as though the game would become a battle of elite defensive units. Defensive back, Dick Anderson intercepted the late great Hall of Fame quarterback, Kenny "the Snake" Stabler, which also resulted in an unfortunate mishap for the Super Bowl champion, Dolphins. Safety, Jake Scott would suffer an injury on the same play, and he would not return to play for the duration of the game. Losing a key member of the defense could become a devastating blow for the morale of the defense.

Scott was a valued member of the Dolphins' secondary at free safety. In hindsight, maybe Scott's absence could have played a significant role at the end of that playoff contest.

Oakland scored its first and only touchdown of the second quarter and first half with a touchdown pass by Stabler.

After halftime of that famed playoff game, there was an increased energy and intensity that both teams would demonstrate. Oakland scored a touchdown pass from Stabler to Hall of Fame wide receiver, Fred Biletnikoff, on a sensational catch he made with one arm that resulted in the star receiver tapping his feet barely in bounds. Miami matched the Raiders' touchdown with a touchdown of their own when Bob Griese threw a 16-yard touchdown pass to wide receiver, Paul Warfield, after a 29-yard pass interference penalty was called against the Raiders on a critical third down.

An extra point block by the Raider's defensive linemen, the late great Bubba Smith only resulted in the Dolphins having a 2- point lead, which was 16-14. The Dolphins through three quarters seemed as though they would acquire a playoff road win. At the beginning of the fourth quarter, Miami's lead increased from 2-points to 5-points, by the score of 19-14, after a 46-yard field goal by the late Dolphins' kicker, Garo Yepremian.

As the fourth quarter progressed, the playoff game between the Miami Dolphins and the Oakland Raiders would become a dramatic seesaw battle. In the last 4:37 seconds of that A.F.C. Divisional Playoff game, the lead between the two teams would change three times. A 72-yard touchdown reception by the late Oakland Raiders Hall of Fame receiver, Cliff Branch gave the Raiders a temporary lead. With 2:08 seconds left, the Dolphins would answer the Raiders' score with a Herculean 23-yard touchdown run by Dolphins running back, Benny Malone, which made the score 26-21 in favor of the Dolphins. With just 24 seconds remaining in the playoff contest, quarterback, Kenny Stabler threw a desperation touchdown pass to Raiders running back, Clarence Davis, while he (Stabler) was in the grasp of Dolphins' defensive end, Vern Den Herder. Davis caught the touchdown pass in the midst of several Miami Dolphin defenders, which would result in the playoff game becoming referred to as "The Sea of Hands", which ended the Dolphins Super Bowl reign.

Great games are what every fan enjoys, especially, if your favorite team is fortunate enough to win. On November 20, 1978, the Monday Night Football game between the Miami Dolphins and the former professional football team, the Houston Oilers, would be considered one of the greatest games featured on Monday Night Football. It was a regular season contest between the upstart Oilers and the perennial playoff powerhouse, the Miami Dolphins.

Though, I was only two weeks removed from my 5th birthday on that winter day in the former home stadium of the Houston Oilers, the Houston Astrodome, I would later see how this one game catapulted the late Oiler's head coach, O.A. "Bum" Phillips, and his Hall of Fame workhorse of a running back, Earl Campbell into the national spotlight. This Monday night game was not a game that ended with a dramatic finish. But what made this game such a devastating loss for Dolphins fans is how this young bruiser of a running back dominated the entire game from the game's inception, as well as until the game's end. Campbell's name was mentioned at nauseam throughout the whole entire night.

In this game, Campbell would prove to my beloved Dolphins, and also the whole entire N.F.L. that he was a new star on the horizon. Of course, in typical Dolphins fashion, the team would draw "first blood" on that uneventful night. Just like the memorable "Sea of Hands" game, the mighty Dolphins would continue to answer the upstart Oilers, score for score, through most of the game.

Both teams were knotted up and tied, 21-21, after three quarters of solid play. When talented Dolphin defender, A.J. Duhe sacked Houston Oilers quarterback, Dan Pastorini in the end zone, which netted a safety, giving the Dolphins a slight lead of 23-21 in the fourth quarter, it might have seemed that the Dolphins would eventually pull out a hard-fought win. The star of that unforgettable game, running back Earl Campbell, answered with a 12-yard touchdown of his own by putting the Oilers back on top by the score of 28-23.

Campbell's score on that short touchdown run would ultimately put the Houston Oilers ahead in that Monday night game for good. If that were not heartbreaking enough, Campbell would cap his coming out game, with a memorable 81-yard rushing touchdown. The Oiler's momentum in that game would never be relinquished, after Campbell's electrifying run.

He (Campbell) ran past, through, and around Dolphin defenders who were literally grasping for air, while trying to tackle the powerful back. Sadly, this game would exploit the Dolphins' defense. This one particular game made the mighty Dolphins look inferior to a team that many thought that the team from South Florida would dominate.

I believe that this one memorable game against a Dolphins' opponent is etched in many football fans and historians' minds that have viewed Monday Night Football. When fans view highlights of past Monday night contests, many fans will see Earl Campbell galloping and outrunning the Dolphins' defense. As much as the game serves as a fond memory for Houston Oilers fans, it will always be one of the games that Dolphins fans will not admire.

January 2, 1982 was the day that one of the most intriguing playoff games took place. Home favorite, and 1981 A.F.C. East champion, the Miami Dolphins and 1981 A.F.C. West champion, San Diego Chargers played in a long, exciting, and dragged out playoff battle. This sensational playoff game was believed to be one of the greatest games of the 1980s, as well as one of the greatest playoff games that have ever been played.

The game was a battle of strengths. Miami's swarming defense finished the 1981 season ranked fifth in the N.F.L. in fewest points allowed. The Dolphins' defense only allowed a total of 27 points in three previous match-ups before this classic playoff contest. San Diego's offense was a different story.

Their offense was ranked tops in the N.F.L. in scoring, passing yards, and total yards. The Chargers offense featured Hall of Fame quarterback, Dan Fouts, Hall of Fame wide receiver, Charlie Joiner, and fellow wide out, Wes Chandler, Pro Bowl running back, Chuck Muncie, talented rookie running back, James Brooks, and Hall of Fame trend setting tight end, Kellen Winslow. Miami's offense, on the other hand, was not as explosive as the Chargers' offensive attack.

The Dolphins' quarterback position featured two quarterbacks, veteran and reserve quarterback, Don Strock, and starting quarterback, the late David Woodley, who both would receive significant playing time, due to both quarterbacks alternating in and out of the starting lineup. They both would become known as "WoodStrock." Miami's offense during that season relied on wide receivers, Jimmy Cefalo and Duriel Harris, and running back Tony Nathan and the late fullback, Andra Franklin were key contributors to Miami's ground game. In the first quarter of the game, San Diego's high- powered offense stunned the Dolphins' defense.

The Chargers scored a barrage of points in that quarter, which was 24 points to be exact. It seemed like my beloved Dolphins would be blown out and embarrassed on their own home turf. Dolphins' fans would soon feel hopeful, when the team answered their own barrage of points in the second quarter with 17 unanswered points. The key play before halftime of that epic game was the hook and lateral play between wide receiver, Duriel Harris and running back, Tony Nathan. Harris caught a pass from Don Strock with six seconds left until halftime, and pitched the ball to Nathan, who would score on a 29-yard touchdown without being touched by any of the Charger's defenders.

Though, the game was played in the winter, the Miami heat proved to be the game's ex-factor. Tight end, Kellen Winslow, battled heat exhaustion, while displaying a dominating performance. He also was the main reason why the Dolphins were not able to complete the comeback.

When the Dolphins had a chance to break the tie with the Chargers, late in the fourth quarter, Kellen Winslow, the "player of the game" blocked the Dolphins' potential game winning field-goal attempt. After this blocked field goal by Winslow, the game was tied, 38-38, and overtime ensued. Soon, the momentum of the game would soon shift from the Dolphins. The Chargers would block another field goal attempt by the Dolphins in overtime. In the end, the game was eventually won in heartbreaking fashion when Chargers' field goal kicker, Rolf Benirschke ended the overtime battle, by the score of 41-38.

Though, I discussed Super Bowl XIX in a previous chapter, in my opinion this game was a heartbreaking loss for me, as well as many other Dolphins fans. I am cognizant of the fact that the game its self was not a close game. The San Francisco 49ers ruined the Dolphins' otherwise magical season with their decisive victory.

As a young Dolphins' fan, I knew in my heart after the second quarter of that game that the 49ers would win the game. While I was viewing the, 38-16, defeat of Marino and the Dolphins, I can recall all of the high scoring games that the Dolphins were a part of during that 1984 season. Leading up to that game, it never crossed my mind that the Dolphins would suffer a lop-sided loss.

I had high hopes that the talented trio of Marino, Duper, and Clayton would continue to display their season long dominance, which was against all of the other N.F.L. defenses they played that year. When I revert back to Super Bowl XIX, the Miami Dolphins during that game looked like a shell of themselves. Both the Miami Dolphins offensive and defensive units did not play as well as they did in the previous playoff games.

Super Bowl XIX, in my opinion, ranks as a heartbreaking loss not just because the Dolphins did not win the game. I believe that the loss was devastating because the team was completely shut down in all facets. It seemed as though the Dolphins could never get anything going all game long. The way that the Dolphins as a team played during that game was foreign to me.

All season long during the Dolphins' 1984 campaign, I had grown accustomed to the Dolphins being the team that dominated their opponents. In the second half of that Super Bowl, the Dolphins did not score a single point. If someone would have told me that the high-flying offense of the Miami Dolphins would only score 16 points in the whole entire game, and be shut out in the second half, I would have said that it would never happen.

That loss was heartbreaking for several reasons. The first reason why the Dolphins' loss to the San Francisco 49ers was so heartbreaking for me as a Dolphins' fan is because the game was supposed to result in Dan Marino and the Dolphins' fairy-tale ending. A second reason why Super Bowl XIX was heartbreaking and difficult to bear was how the protection from the Dolphins' offensive line could not withstand the 49ers relentless pass- rush.

Seeing Marino sacked four times during that Super Bowl, when he was not sacked at all in the previous Dolphins' playoff victories really made me feel disappointed and sad. On the defensive side of the ball, I can recall how the Dolphins' defense looked far from stellar and outstanding. The defense could not stop Hall of Fame quarterback, Joe Montana and the 49ers offense.

Montana threw 2 touchdowns, while rushing for 1, and running back/fullback, Roger Craig became the game's breakout star. Marino, on the other hand, only managed to throw for 1 touchdown the entire game. The highlight that is always embedded in my mind after that heartbreaking Dolphins' defeat is when Roger Craig scored the final touchdown of that game by high-kneeing it in the end zone for a score.

1985 was supposed to be the year that the Miami Dolphins would avenge their Super Bowl loss the previous year. It also was a significant season for the Dolphins franchise because it was the franchise's 20th season. The Dolphins still had the talented offensive trio of Marino, Duper, and Clayton still taking the N.F.L. by storm.

Though, Marino did not have as good of a year in 1985 as he had in the previous season, the season was still an overall success. There were distractions in the Dolphins' 1985 campaign. Star quarterback and the National Football League's Most Valuable Player, Dan Marino, had a contract dispute with the team and held out in the off- season. More adversity ensued before the 1985 season when Marino's other favorite passing target, Mark Duper was injured.

The team as a whole got off to a shaky start in the 1985 season. Through nine games, the Dolphins had a 5-4 record. At that point in the season, the Dolphins were a third place team.

A.F.C. East divisional rivals, the New York Jets and the New England Patriots improved drastically. Both teams would finish the 1985 season with an 11-5 record, while also qualifying for the playoffs. The New York Jets would finish the season in second place in the A.F.C. East, just ahead of the New England Patriots because the Jets had a better divisional and conference record than the Patriots.

The Miami Dolphins, on the other hand, captured their third consecutive A.F.C. divisional title by season's end. Due to the Dolphins' 7- game win streak to end the 1985 regular season, the Dolphins were positioning themselves as a contender out of the A.F.C. to represent the conference in yet another Super Bowl appearance. With the Dolphins' impressive Monday Night victory over the eventual Super Bowl champions, the Chicago Bears, the Dolphins seemed poised to play in a rematch in the Superdome in New Orleans.

Miami came into the A.F.C. Championship game poised and confident to make another Super Bowl. Most N.F.L. commentators thought that the Dolphins would win the A.F.C. conference, yet again. On Sunday, January 12, 1986, the Dolphins would suffer an upset at home in the Orange Bowl against the eventual Super Bowl runner-up, the New England Patriots. I vividly remember how this game was played in the rain.

As a Dolphins fan, I was anticipating another Dolphins' win. Sadly, on that miserable rainy day in South Florida, the Dolphins would not be fortunate enough to reach the ultimate game. The Patriots defense and running game aided the upset win over my Miami Dolphins, 31-14.

The Dolphins committed 6 turnovers, which sealed the Patriots victory. After watching the game, I remember how disappointed I felt when the Dolphins' season ended unceremoniously. That game was heartbreaking as a Dolphins fan due to the high expectations that were set by the media for the Dolphins to reach Super Bowl XX.

Memorable games in the N.F.L. are played each passing season. The regular season game between the visiting Miami Dolphins and the New York Jets is still a game for the ages. As a fan of high scoring football games and offensive football, the 1986 contest between these two divisional rivals served as a treat for me, although I did not like the final result of that game.

The Jets quarterback, Ken O'Brien and Dolphins great, Dan Marino played in an offensive tug-of-war. Though, O'Brien did not enjoy the same prolonged success as Dan Marino, on that September day, O'Brien and the Jets outlasted my beloved Dolphins. This contest between these A.F.C. divisional rivals set single game records in combined net yards (884), and combined touchdown passes (10), which now has since been broken. Marino had one of his signature games by throwing for six scoring tosses.

Though, the Dolphins were defeated, the game provided a plethora of memories and entertainment for the casual N.F.L. fan. I remember Duper and Clayton also having monstrous receiving games. Duper had 154 yards, while Clayton also had a sensational performance with 174 yards.

The divisional foe, New York Jets had a strong performance from wide receiver, Wesley Walker, who caught all four passing touchdowns that quarterback, Ken O'Brien threw. Walker had a Hall of Fame caliber day. He single-handedly roasted the Dolphins secondary.

This game featured the offensive, talented, trio of Marino, Duper, and Clayton at their best. It was a seesaw battle that I thought would eventually result in a memorable win for the Dolphins, but the star of the game, Wesley Walker, became a nuisance by catching the tying touchdown reception to send the game into overtime.

At that point, the score was 45-45. In many instances, during an N.F.L. contest, momentum can carry a team into victory. The Jets definitely had both confidence and momentum when Walker scored the tying touchdown with no time left on the clock, at the end of regulation.

When I saw the highlights of that game on television, I remember how the commentator kept breaking in during the game that I was viewing locally that the Dolphins were on top, and then he would say that the Jets took the lead. I thought that the Dolphins would seek out a win when they took a 45-38, lead in the fourth quarter. As regulation ended and Jets wide receiver, Wesley Walker scored on a game-tying touchdown, I can vividly remember how I had an uneasy feeling when I saw him score again.

My gut feeling was telling me that the Dolphins defense did not have an answer as to how to impede or stop the Jets receiver from embarrassing them. It was one thing to give up a touchdown, but giving up the tying score at the end of regulation to force overtime was definitely a cause for concern. Once overtime ensued, the "killer of the Dolphins' secondary" caught the game clinching touchdown reception, and it resulted in a heartbreaking, 51-45, overtime loss for the offensive explosive, Dolphins.

Free agency commenced in the 1992 season, and the Miami Dolphins would sign one of the most coveted free agents during that season. Former Green Bay Packers and perennial Pro-Bowl, tight end, Keith Jackson, signed a hefty new contract with the Miami Dolphins. Receivers, Mark Duper and Mark Clayton were at this point, 11 and 10- year veterans, respectively.

I can recall how this was supposed to be the talented trio of Marino, Duper, and Clayton's last hoorah. It was reported and rumored in the media that the Dolphins would ultimately move on from the talented receiver pair, by season's end. The team's response to the eventual departure of the Marks Brothers resulted in a successful season, although, the Dolphins did not win the Super Bowl that year.

The 1992 season was a success, in my opinion, for a several reasons. One reason why the year of 1992 should be remembered as a success is what the Dolphins and the region of South Florida had to endure before the start of that season. A Category 5 Atlantic hurricane, named Hurricane Andrew, devastated the state of Florida, as well as some parts of Louisiana in August of 1992. The storm was during that time one of the costliest storms financial wise in United States history.

Miami-Dade and Broward counties suffered extreme loss and devastation of homes, businesses, as well as a plethora of property damage throughout the region. Because of the hurricane, I can recall how close it was to affecting the Miami Dolphins home games at what was formerly known as, Joe Robbie Stadium. Eventually, the Dolphins were able to play their full schedule without having any lingering effects from Hurricane Andrew.

Another reason why the 1992 season was successful for my beloved Dolphins is because they were able to win the A.F.C. East title. And of course, lastly, that 1992 team would finish one game from playing in the Super Bowl.

When I viewed that A.F.C. Championship game in my dorm room, I was thankful that I was alone. Before that game, I thought that the A.F.C. Championship would result in a Dolphins' victory and the franchises' sixth Super Bowl berth, but on that clear 75-degree day in Miami, a Super Bowl berth for the Miami Dolphins was just not meant to be. It was a game that was sad on a plethora of fronts, as a loyal and committed Dolphins' fan and enthusiast. Just like in other previous big games, like Super Bowl XIX, the Dolphins could not find a way to come out of an important game, victorious.

All throughout that game, I vividly recall how Hall of Fame Buffalo Bills running back, Thurman Thomas would catch a plethora of screen passes, which the Dolphins' defense could not stop. It seemed like on every down, Thomas was getting the ball. On offense, the Dolphins did not fare much better.

Marino was intercepted twice, and the Dolphins' rushing game only produced 33 yards in the whole entire game. I personally rank this particular loss 2nd behind the Super Bowl XIX loss in the Marino era. The 29 to 10 loss to the divisional rival and eventual Super Bowl runner-up, Buffalo Bills, would essentially become the closest that quarterback Dan Marino, wide receivers Mark Duper, and Mark Clayton would come to making another Super Bowl appearance in their stellar careers, which is extremely disappointing and sad.

After appearing in the 1992 A.F.C. Championship game against the Buffalo Bills, I was hopeful that the Miami Dolphins could build on that success. The 1993 season got off to a promising start after the departures of wide receivers, Mark Duper and Mark Clayton. Miami commenced the season with a 3-1 record, until the worst case scenario occurred in the former Cleveland Stadium.

Star quarterback and face of the Miami Dolphins' franchise, Dan Marino ruptured his Achilles' tendon in that Dolphins win over the Cleveland Browns. As a fan, I knew that the Dolphins had a tough road to climb after Marino's injury. By the end of the 1993 season, three different starting quarterbacks had the task of trying to fill the shoes of Dan Marino.

Scott Mitchell, the Dolphins' backup quarterback, filled in admirably in Marino's absence. Mitchell lead the Dolphins to a 9-2 record, before he, too was replaced, due to injury. Sadly, for the Dolphins, the team's chances of a playoff berth rested in the hands of a third-string quarterback, the former Super Bowl winning coach of the Philadelphia Eagles, Doug Pederson, and long-time veteran quarterback, Steve Deberg.

One of the great moments of that 1993 season for the Miami Dolphins was the Thanksgiving victory, a 16 to 14, win over the eventual Super Bowl champion, Dallas Cowboys, which was won in the former Texas Stadium in frigid weather. Unfortunately, this victory would be the last victory that the Dolphins would enjoy for the rest of that season. Miami would go on to lose five consecutive games, after a promising victory on the road, over a Super Bowl caliber team.

For the Dolphins, the magic number to qualify for the playoffs that season was 1. The team had five chances to earn at least one victory to become participants of the 1993 post-season. On the last day of the regular season, the Dolphins only had to beat the last place team in their division, the New England Patriots, to at least earn a playoff Wild Card spot.

Sometimes, in sports, last place teams who do not have any incentive to win, or anything to play for, typically, become spoilers. On that January day, just a day after New Year's Day in 1994, for this Dolphins fan, the New Year began in a negative fashion, after a heartbreaking end of the regular season loss to the lowly Patriots. Miami had to convert a fourth quarter field goal by kicker, Pete Stoyanovich, just to send the game into overtime.

After the end of regulation, the visiting Dolphins and the home Patriots were tied, 27 to 27. But in overtime, the Dolphins would suffer a heartbreaking loss, after New England Patriots quarterback, Drew Bledsoe, threw the game winning, 36-yard touchdown pass to wide receiver, Michael Timpson, to break the tie, and win, 33 to 27, over coach Shula and the Marino-less, Dolphins. The 1993 season began with tremendous promise, but ultimately, it ended in dramatic and devastating fashion, which had many Dolphins fans wondering, "What might have been if Dan Marino did not suffer a season-long injury?"

Resiliency is what in my opinion, describes the 1994 Miami Dolphins. I believe that the team was resilient because it bounced back from not being able to qualify for the playoffs in the team's prior season, to a playoff berth in the following campaign. What I noticed about that team was the fact that the team did not suffer any blowout losses in any of the team's six defeats.

The worst loss that the Dolphins suffered that season was an 11-point, high scoring loss to the Buffalo Bills, 42 to 31.

Miami would also capture another A.F.C. East divisional title with a 10 win and six- loss record.

Quarterback, Dan Marino was the epitome of resilience when he returned from his Achilles tendon injury, by playing to his Pro-Bowl caliber form and potential. Marino earned several honors that season. The eventual Hall of Fame quarterback earned the 1994 Comeback Player of the Year award, the 1994 UPI AFL-AFC Player of the Year honor, an A.F.C. Pro-Bowl selection, as well as earning an All-Pro selection.

After making the playoffs that season, the Marino led Dolphins were able to secure a home playoff victory against the Montana led Kansas City Chiefs, 27 to 17. The team would then have a date with the former team, known as the San Diego Chargers, on the Chargers' home turf, the following week. Marino and the Dolphins began that playoff game by jumping out to a 21 to 6 lead over quarterback, Stan Humphries and the Chargers.

What I remember most about this heartbreaking and disappointing playoff game is how San Diego and Miami played a game of two halves. Miami got off to a sizzling start in the first half, but in the second half, the team was cold. Marino and the Dolphins would not score a single point in the second half, for the rest of that playoff game.

Though, the Chargers did not score in the first quarter, they were able to score with consistency in the ensuing quarters. Also, I can recall during that game how the Chargers were just "chipping away" at the Dolphins' lead. It was frustrating to see how the Chargers were having relatively good success on offense, with the running of power back, Natrone Means, who ran over the Dolphins' defense for 139 yards, while also scoring on a 24-yard touchdown run.

When the Chargers' ground game became effective, I specifically remember thinking how the Chargers' run game was keeping Marino on the sidelines, and how the battle of time of possession could play a significant role in the Dolphins coming out on the wrong side of the game. Miami's time of possession was 20:40, while San Diego's time of possession was nearly two times as much as the Dolphins. Because San Diego enjoyed an enormous amount of ground control, their time of possession was 39:20.

The Dolphins did not lose that game because of Dan Marino, because the quarterback was not intercepted once in that game. I believe that the turning point and the momentum changed in that game in the third quarter when former Dolphins running back, Bernie Parmalee, was tackled in the end zone by Chargers defensive tackle, Reuben Davis, for a safety. At the end of the game, the Dolphins would lose in a Hollywood-style ending when Dolphins kicker, Pete Stoyanovich missed a potential game-winning 47-yard field goal that would have put the Dolphins back on top, at the end of regulation.

Discussing painful losses is not what I would prefer to discuss as a Dolphins fan. I am certain that there are other significant losses that other Dolphins fans might consider heartbreaking. Whether you as a fan of the Dolphins agree or disagree, the last heartbreaking loss that I will discuss, occurred in the 2000 regular season on Monday Night Football.

When this game occurred, it was the franchise's first season since 1982 that the Miami Dolphins franchise would play without Dolphins great, Dan Marino. The 2000 Dolphins were extremely formidable on defense. By season's end, the Dolphins would have five defensive starters elected to the Pro-Bowl.

Miami would enjoy another successful season by winning the A.F.C. East title, while also making their 20th playoff appearance. Jay Fiedler was the team's starting quarterback in the post-Marino era. The Dolphins defense was led by a plethora of defensive standouts. Hall of Fame defensive end, Jason Taylor, and fellow defensive end, Trace Armstrong manned the first wave of the defensive. Hall of Fame linebacker, Zach Thomas, was a tremendous and solid defender, and defensive backs, Sam Madison, Patrick Surtain, and Brock Marion, covered and patrolled the back half of the defense.

On a clear and cool Monday night in East Rutherford, New Jersey, the Miami Dolphins would again become participants of another classic game against the divisional rival, New York Jets. The quarterback battle between both teams was basically a draw. Dolphins' quarterback, Jay Fiedler would throw three interceptions in the game, while opposing quarterback, Vinny Testaverde would also throw the same amount of passing picks.

Every game is played through all four quarters, and unfortunately for the Miami Dolphins, they only played three on that cool October night. The Dolphins were enjoying a blowout win in the contest's first three quarters. They were ahead 30 to 7, and I can still remember being one of the millions of Monday Night Football viewers who had retired to bed, thinking that the Dolphins would earn a blowout victory.

The New York Jets somehow turned it on in the fourth quarter when many in America either tuned away from the game, or fell asleep because on the East coast, the game did not end until past midnight. In other words, a winner was not determined until Tuesday morning, after the Jets scored a barrage of points in the fourth quarter, to send an other wise lop-sided game into overtime. Vinny and the Jets would score 30 frantic points in the fourth quarter, in order to force the game into overtime.

The very next morning when I heard that the Jets had won the game, I was initially surprised and shocked. It was 30 to 7 in the Dolphins favor when I fell asleep. I never thought that the Dolphins defensive unit would allow the Jets to score that many points in the fourth quarter. Sadly, when the dust settled on that Monday/Tuesday night game, the Dolphins would be defeated, 40-37, in overtime, in one of the greatest games in Monday Night Football history. This game, which is commonly referred to as, "The Monday Night Miracle" is the example of a team losing in heartbreak fashion.

CHAPTER 5
The Search to Replace Dan Marino

Just like the Dolphins' difficulties in trying to replace legendary coach, Don Shula, the replacement for Hall of Fame quarterback, Dan Marino, have also been difficult over the years. Marino last played in an injury-plagued season of 1999. Statistically, the season was not one of his best.

Although, the Dolphins would complete the 1999 regular season with 9 wins and 7 losses, the season did not end on a positive note. Sure, Marino and the Dolphins would enjoy winning a Wildcard Playoff game in Seattle in the 1999 postseason, but the following week against the Jacksonville Jaguars would be the stellar and illustrious quarterback's final game. Unfortunately, that game would not only be the final time that Marino would be the starting quarterback for the Miami Dolphins, but it would also become the most lopsided defeat in Marino's career, as well as in Dolphins' postseason history.

After watching that game, I felt really bad for Marino. He did not get the chance to atone for that devastating playoff loss. Sadly, some casual fans viewing that game might only remember that horrendous defeat.

It was after that lackluster playoff game that the Dolphins franchise was set to move on from the quarterback who gave all of his passion, energy, and heart to this one professional football organization. Fourth year and Hall of Fame coach, Jimmy Johnson would also retire after the 1999 season. The subsequent coach after coach Johnson was coach Dave Wannstedt.

According to his assessment of Marino, he felt that Marino should also retire. Now I can recall how teams such as, the Minnesota Vikings and my native, hometown team, the New Orleans Saints were rumored to be interested in the Hall of Fame quarterback's services. I am sure that the talented quarterback was tempted to show all the critics and doubters that he could still throw the football with great velocity, and could also win more games.

On March 13, 2000, the Miami Dolphins' leader in quarterback victories, passing yards, and touchdown passes retired from the National Football League. In hindsight, I believe that Dan Marino still had a lot of football left in him. He would never get the chance to display that golden arm again.

As a loyal Dolphins fan and enthusiast, of course, I wanted to see the Dolphins great suit up for another season. I remember thinking that it was not fair that Marino really did not get the chance to retire when he truly wanted to. His retirement came from the suggestion of close family members and others.

Today, when I see various quarterbacks play the game well into the 40s, I think of Dan Marino. He retired at the age of 38 as the quarterback with the most N.F.L. victories without winning a Super Bowl with 155 wins. I believe that the Miami Dolphins have not enjoyed years of consistency due to the inadequacies and errors in trying to find a quarterback who is just as gifted and talented in leadership and throwing the football as Dan Marino was.

It is definitely true what they say about quarterback play in the National Football League. Many say that if a team does not have a good and competent starting quarterback, then the team will suffer. Since legendary quarterback, Dan Marino retired in 2000 the Miami Dolphins have had 23 different starting quarterbacks behind the center.

Marino spoiled Dolphins fans with his longevity and mobility. The quarterback was not the most mobile of quarterbacks to ever have played the position. His damage was done on opposing defenses with his quick release, and his ability to elude defensive lineman and pass rushers in the pocket. The Hall of Fame quarterback was an "Iron man" when he played.

He suited up week after week for the Miami Dolphins from the time he was inserted into the starting lineup in 1983, until his Achilles tendon injury in week six of the 1993 regular season. No one can dispute how amazing that streak was. In the N.F.L., a quarterback is asked to do a lot.

Most starting quarterbacks are expected to show up on the field, week after week. Fans expect the starting quarterback to play for their respective teams, rain or shine. But what many fans and experts do not realize is how difficult it is for a starting quarterback to endure all of the bumps and bruises and media scrutiny that the most visible face of the franchise, other than the head coach, endures.

This is why the quarterback position is so important. He has to know how to be able to play well, consistently lead, and also avoid serious injuries. Injuries are a part of the game of football.

Usually, not many players can go through one season, if not years of being unscathed or unaffected by pain. The Dolphins had less than a hand full of quarterbacks who played in the post-Marino era that were above average starters. Quarterback, Damon Huard, I thought was a good quarterback, who backed up Marino.

In my opinion, he played well enough to succeed the great quarterback (Marino) after posting a 4-1 record when he started in Marino's place when Marino was injured in his final season with the Dolphins. I wonder how the Dolphins would have fared had Huard become the Dolphins starting quarterback in 2000. We will never know because quarterback, Jay Fiedler was ultimately promoted in to the starting role.

Fiedler was a decent quarterback for the Miami Dolphins. He helped the team win 10 plus games in three of his four seasons with the aqua and orange. Fiedler also has the distinction of being the last Dolphins quarterback to earn a playoff victory, in the Dolphins 2000 Wild Card overtime win versus the Indianapolis Colts. Who knows how successful he would have become in his career with the Dolphins if running back, Ricky Williams, did not abruptly retire before the start of the 2004 season. Another quarterback who demonstrated great promise was Chad Pennington. In 2008, he led the Miami Dolphins to an A.F.C. East title and playoff berth, before a nagging shoulder injury eventually sidelined him for good, thus ending and derailing his potentially promising career.

Failed physicals occur all the time in the N.F.L. Each of the 32 N.F.L. franchises have team doctors who are responsible for administering tests on injuries that each player might suffer during the course of that player's season or career. Former San Diego Charger and former New Orleans Saint, and future Hall of Fame quarterback, Drew Brees was a failed physical away from helping the Miami Dolphins carry on its tradition of Hall of Fame quarterbacks.

Now I understand that one player does not have all the influence and power to help a team win, but Drew Brees has shown throughout his 20 seasons in the N.F.L., with 15 of them being with the New Orleans Saints that he was the difference maker between the two franchises. That failed physical that was determined by Dolphins team doctors changed the trajectory of the Dolphins, as well as the Saints organizations. As a native of New Orleans, I am familiar with the losing culture and the team history of the New Orleans Saints.

Upon the arrival of quarterback, Drew Brees, the Saints' franchise was never considered among the National Football League's elite. In fact, the New Orleans Saints franchise has the distinction of having twenty straight losing seasons. The Miami Dolphins on the other hand would enjoy a plethora of winning and enjoyable seasons in its rich history, while winning two Lombardy trophies.

Immediately, the Saints transformed into a perennial playoff and Super Bowl contender when Brees became the Saints starting quarterback. The very first season of the Brees era in New Orleans, the Saints would win the N.F.C. South title, earn a playoff berth, and go to the franchises' first of three N.F.C. Championship games. 2009, was the year that the New Orleans Saints would see the Dolphin's pass on Brees, ultimately, pay a huge reward.

In week 7 of the 2009 season, Brees and the Saints played a high scoring regular season game against my Miami Dolphins. The Saints trailed the Dolphins 24 to 3 in the second quarter of that game. Though, statistically the game would not be Brees' best, he did contribute to the game by rushing for two touchdowns, as the Saints would mount a dramatic comeback.

Sadly, for the Dolphins, they could not hold on to their big halftime lead at home. Brees would make the Dolphins pay for not overlooking that failed physical by winning the game 46 to 34. The quarterback was not finished telling the Dolphins through his outstanding play that the organization made a crucial mistake by not signing him.

Super Bowl XLIV was played in the Dolphins' home stadium, which is now referred to as Hard Rock Stadium in

Miami Gardens, Florida. Ironically, the New Orleans Saints would defeat the Indianapolis Colts in the franchise's one and only Super Bowl appearance and victory. Though, the Saints would not make it to the Super Bowl again in the Drew Brees led era, his steady play helped thrust the New Orleans Saints organization into elite status, while he was the team's quarterback. When he retired at the end of the 2020 season, Brees owned and shared many of the N.F.L. records at the quarterback position. As a loyal and devoted Dolphins fan, I wonder where would the Dolphins be as an organization and franchise if Drew Brees were the Dolphins' starting quarterback.

Bob Griese and Dan Marino were special quarterbacks for the Miami Dolphins in two different N.F.L. eras. Griese was a talented quarterback in his own right. To many of the N.F.L. insiders during the Griese era for the Miami Dolphins, the Hall of Fame quarterback was specifically known for his cool demeanor and intelligence on and off the field.

Marino was known as the Dolphins' fiery competitor. I have never seen a quarterback, with the exception of future Hall of Fame quarterback, Tom Brady, play the game with such conviction and passion, since Dan Marino. Like the late great coach, Don Shula, Marino was emotional and animated.

He wanted the football in his hands in the fourth quarter. As a fan of the Dolphins for approximately 40 years, I have seen the magic of Dan Marino, first hand. Aside from all of the gaudy statistics that Marino amassed during his playing days with the Miami Dolphins, he in many of his years with the organization willed and put the team on his broad shoulders.

The Hall of Fame quarterback was a winner and had a flare for the dramatic. Since, Marino's retirement, his legacy has not had the slightest hint of becoming challenged. No one can say that a quarterback is the next Dan Marino because they'll never be anyone like him.

After Marino did not get a chance to retire the way he would have liked, the Dolphins have not been able to enjoy the excitement and success they had when Marino was leading the team. A lesson that I have learned from all of the quarterbacks who played post-Marino era is that the starting quarterback position in the National Football League is likened to a spouse whom one might choose.

When an individual initially marries, he or she has the potential to remain with one's spouse for a lifetime. In regard to a marriage, it is not an exact science. One would hope that there would be more good days than not so good ones.

Although, playing the game of football is limited and does not last a lifetime, choosing a starting quarterback that could play over ten years or more in the N.F.L. can be viewed as a lifetime commitment. Thus far, none of the starting quarterbacks who have played post- Marino have been able to reach the commitment status, according to Miami Dolphin standards. As I previously stated and discussed, the only Dolphins quarterback to come close to winning consistently with the Miami Dolphins was Jay Fiedler, and the Dolphins organization during the quarterback's tenure, only committed to him for four seasons. (Currently, quarterback Tua Tagovailoa is displaying consistency in winning potential).

The legacy of a franchise is in many cases solidified with the quarterback position. If an N.F.L. organization desires to become mentioned in the same breath as other winning teams and franchises in history and around the league, then the quarterback play must be superb. An N.F.L. organization is fortunate when the right quarterback is either taken in the draft, or acquired by free agency. Hopefully, the Miami Dolphins will once again enjoy the National Football League's version of success when talking about Dan Marino's replacement becomes non-existent.

Year after year since Dan Marino retired, as a fan I have been waiting for a quarterback to help resurrect the franchise.

For seventeen wonderful years, the Miami Dolphins relied on the outstanding quarterback play of Marino. He brought fans into the stands in what was formerly known as the Orange Bowl Stadium, as well as Joe Robbie and Pro Player Stadium.

There has not been a quarterback since Marino that has "wowed" fans with their outstanding play on a consistent basis. The Dolphins have not drafted many quarterbacks in the first round. Instead, the franchise for many years have elected to rely on veteran free agents to play what is arguably the most important position in all of football.

As I watched the Miami Dolphins over the years, the organization has not had real consistency at the quarterback position. It seemed as though for years, the Dolphins have basically been unsuccessful when it comes to having a viable quarterback as the starter. Because of the uncertainty at the position, sadly, the franchise has not been able to enjoy consistency in winning playoff games.

Now, I am not saying that some of the starting quarterbacks for the Miami Dolphins did not have relatively good games from time to time. In the N.F.L., anyone is capable of having a breakout game. What has eluded the Dolphins franchise for a plethora of years is a quarterback that has the capability of taking over a game on a consistent basis.

Since Dan Marino retired, there has been only one quarterback that was elected to the Pro Bowl, and that is current, quarterback, Tua Tagovailoa. Sure, there have been quarterbacks who started for the Miami Dolphins in the past that had N.F.L. talent, but they did not possess the type of talent that would cause fans and others to experience the same success as the Marino-era. I believe that the Miami Dolphins are gradually becoming a franchise of consistent winning with Tagovailoa as the starter.

The defensive side of the ball has had a plethora of Pro Bowl players since the retirement of Dan Marino. On offense, there have been other positions, such as the running back position and the wide receiver position that has at least made one Pro Bowl. With the drafting of Tua Tagovailoa, fifth in the 2020 at quarterback, the state of the Dolphins' franchise, and search for Dan Marino's replacement looks promising.

It is not that simple to either discover or find a quarterback to help bring the Miami Dolphins into one of the elite teams jockeying for playoff or Super Bowl contention. For approximately 20 years, the Miami Dolphins have not enjoyed a quarterback who could get the team "over the hump." Tua Tagovailoa does not have to be the next Dan Marino, but have his own identity when it comes to playing winning football.

One thing that a winning quarterback must have is a competitive instinct. He must not become satisfied with average. My hope for the Dolphins franchise is that current quarterback, Tua Tagovailoa can become the effective competitor at quarterback on the team that has given him the opportunity to become successful.

Success for many N.F.L. teams starts and ends with a leader at quarterback. The quarterback must have an undeniable will to win. Although, the Dolphins' quarterback position has had glimpses of success, prolonged success has not occurred.

If it were just that simple to find a starting quarterback to play inspired football for a significant amount of time, then the Miami Dolphins would have already been considered among the NFL's elite franchises. Special talent at the quarterback position requires both time and patience. Dolphin fans have not had any other choice but to remain hopeful and patient that one day the quarterback position will return to the glory of the past. There is a certain swagger that elite quarterbacks play with.

Dan Marino always played with extreme swagger and confidence. He always knew that with his quick release and powerful arm, the Dolphins were always within striking distance to take the lead in the fourth quarter. A quarterback can have all the tools and mechanics to be an N.F.L. caliber quarterback, but on the N.F.L. level, he has to have more than the right build or arm talent.

Many who have seen Dan Marino play, are aware of what he could do, just with his right arm, alone. I was always amazed how Marino could win so many games without being the fastest, or even the greatest athlete on the field. It was his will, confidence, and determination not to lose that helped Marino last in the N.F.L. for so many years and seasons.

As a fan, I can tell that when it came to playing football, Marino was in his element. When an individual is passionate about playing and winning, it could have an infectious effect. Teammates typically respond favorably when the quarterback is fearless and passionate about winning.

In the N.F.L., of course talent is required. There are other intangibles that an individual who desires to succeed at the quarterback position must have. For starters, he must love every aspect of the game of professional football in order to experience any type of prolonged success in the league.

Secondly, he has to be "all in" when it comes to playing for a franchise and organization, such as, the Miami Dolphins. Thirdly, the quarterback who desires to have any type of success must have a vision for him and the team. And lastly, the individual must be a self- starter and motivator.

In my opinion, talent is important at the quarterback position, but it is not the only thing that a quarterback must have to become as successful as Dan Marino was on the gridiron. Marino played and overcame many knee injuries. I can recall the plethora of surgeries he had when it was reported that he would have his knee scoped in the off- season. Marino loved being the quarterback of the Miami Dolphins, even when the team and organization encountered tremendous adversity on and off the field. An individual who desires to have a successful career for the Miami Dolphins at quarterback must forge his own path to greatness, which will result in success, with the right passion and mindset.

Reliable quarterbacks are each N.F.L. team's desire. In the present N.F.L., most teams do not have the patience to wait if a starting quarterback will develop. Unlike 10 to 20 years ago, some teams would draft a quarterback in the first round and feel obligated to remain with him just because they (the team) invested so much in that particular player.

There is a little bit of luck when an N.F.L. team hits the "jackpot" on a starting quarterback. In regard to Marino, the Dolphins also lucked out on picking him. According to many of the Dolphins' brass in the 1983 draft, the Dolphins were not looking for a quarterback.

In fact, the team was looking for another defensive end to help solidify the defense. The Dolphins seemed content to remain with incumbent starter, the late David Woodley, who was a young quarterback at the time. He also led the Dolphins to the Super Bowl in the previous year, though it resulted in a Super Bowl loss against the former N.F.L. team then known as the Washington Redskins.

No one can ever say for certain how a player's career will pan out. The Miami Dolphins when they picked Marino late in the first round of the 1983 draft had a potential quarterback controversy brewing. Here you have a young quarterback in David Woodley who just took your franchise to the ultimate game, the Super Bowl, and sitting on the bench is another young quarterback who has everything that a team would want in regard to the makeup of a franchise signal caller.

This quarterback scenario was a prime example back in 1983 for the Miami Dolphins of how important and vital it is for an N.F.L. organization to have the right fit at starting quarterback. Before Marino was ever considered as a draft pick for the Miami Dolphins, the franchise enjoyed many other seasons of success. The Dolphins at the time of Marino's arrival did not have a pressing quarterback need.

If a team feels that it can upgrade at any position, they will not hesitate to eventually make that move. When it came to either inserting Woodley or Marino into the starting lineup, after week five of the 1983 season, I am certain that the Miami Dolphins were not aware that Dan Marino would elevate many of his teammate's play with that confident assurance and swagger that would be a mainstay for the Miami Dolphins for almost two decades. Quarterback play that is superb and outstanding for many years could sometimes put an N.F.L. franchise at a disadvantage.

How does the team prepare for the great quarterback's eventual exit? I believe that the Miami Dolphins were not initially thinking about Marino's successor prior to the 1999 season. In 1998, Marino started all 16 regular season games, and led the Dolphins to a 10-6 record and a spot in the playoffs. His statistics were still solid.

At 37 years of age, which is mature by N.F.L. standards, Marino still threw 23 touchdown passes and over 3,000 passing yards without any signs of slowing down. Some quarterbacks who were half of Marino's age could not compare with his statistical prowess. Though, the quarterback remained a vital asset to the Dolphins' offense, no one saw the next season as the Hall of Fame quarterback's last.

2012 commenced the Ryan Tannehill era in Miami. He was the first quarterback that the Dolphins would choose in the first round since the drafting of Dan Marino in the 1983. Tannehill was drafted 8th in the 2012 draft.

The quarterback out of Texas A&M was supposed to help resurrect the Dolphins franchise from mediocrity to a competitive one. Tannehill showed glimpses of his potential while he was under center for the Dolphins. There were games that he looked like a reliable starter for the team, and then there were other times that he did not play to his potential.

Statistically speaking, Tannehill broke some Dolphin records. As a rookie he demonstrated great promise when he surpassed Dolphin great, Dan Marino's single game rookie passing yard record by throwing for 431 yards in a 24 to 21, overtime loss to the Arizona Cardinals in week 4 of the 2012 season. After the completion of that season, Tannehill would set Miami Dolphin rookie records for passing yards, attempts, and completions.

2016 was the quarterback's best season in completion percentage when he finished the season with a career high completion percentage of 67.1. This would also be his finest season as the starting quarterback for the Miami Dolphins. Tannehill contributed to the Dolphins enjoying their first playoff berth and 10-win season since 2008.

After a left leg injury sidelined him for the entire 2017 N.F.L. season, the quarterback returned to the starting quarterback role in the 2018 N.F.L. regular season. It was during that 2018 campaign that Tannehill was a part of the "Miracle in Miami," which resulted in a victory for the Miami Dolphins over the divisional rival, New England Patriots, 34 to 33, on the last play of the game. He began that exciting play with a pass over the middle to former Dolphin wide receiver, Kenny Stills, who then pitched the ball to another former Dolphin wide receiver, DeVante Parker at midfield. After Parker tossed the ball to former Dolphin running back, Kenyan Drake, the running back then ran the ball for a 52-yard touchdown to help seal the victory.

Sadly, this would become the highlight of Tannehill's stint with the Miami Dolphins. In 2019, the quarterback was traded to the Tennessee Titans. During his time with the Dolphins, Tannehill took a plethora of sacks.

There were some instances that the offensive line was responsible for the quarterback's plethora of sacks to the opposing defenders, but in many cases, Tannehill held on to the ball too long. In the genesis of his career with the Dolphins, I was hoping that he would correct his inconsistent play. The quarterback would play approximately six full seasons with the organization.

Tannehill never reached his full potential as the starting quarterback for the Miami Dolphins. This is why the Dolphins chose to trade him to the Tennessee Titans on draft night in 2019. Tannehill never worked out in Miami, which essentially made him expendable.

As I previously stated, Tua Tagovailoa was selected 5th overall in the first round of the 2020 N.F.L. draft by the Miami Dolphins. He was a productive college quarterback for the powerhouse college football team, the Alabama Crimson Tide. Tagovailoa initially got his chance to break into the mighty Crimson Tide lineup when he replaced incumbent starter, Jalen Hurts in the second half of the 2018 College Football Playoff National Championship game against the Georgia Bulldogs, due to Hurt's ineffective play. The quarterback threw the game winning 41-yard touchdown that helped Alabama earn their 17th National Championship, with a 26 to 23 victory as a true freshman.

Tagovailoa had a successful sophomore campaign, although the Crimson Tide would eventually lose the National Championship game against the Clemson Tigers. In his junior year, it began successfully, but injuries would soon plague the talented quarterback's season. Tagovailoa and the Crimson Tide were on their way to another successful and productive season when disaster struck.

Unfortunately, the former Tide quarterback suffered significant and career threatening injuries in a win against SEC opponent, Mississippi State Bulldogs. Tagovailoa would have a dislocated hip, while also fracturing the posterior wall, as well as a concussion and broken nose. The injury that the quarterback suffered could have affected his chances of having a career in the N.F.L.

When the Miami Dolphins took Tagovailoa in the 2020 draft, there were questions concerning the quarterback's ability to regain his outstanding form before the devastating hip injury. The former coach of the Dolphins, coach Brian Flores, did not want to insert the talented quarterback in the starting lineup, until he thought that the quarterback's dislocated hip injury was stable enough to endure the rigors of the N.F.L. Tagovailoa was projected as the first overall selection of the entire draft before the hip injury threatened his overall draft status.

The left-handed Alabama product drew comparisons to fellow left-hand and Hall of Fame quarterback, former Tampa Bay Buccaneer and former San Francisco 49er, Super Bowl winning quarterback, Steve Young. Tagovailoa's rookie campaign for the Miami Dolphins was a relatively successful one. He started nine games for the Fins, while compiling a starting record of 6 wins and only 3 losses.

In my opinion, the Dolphins have the potential of gaining another productive starting quarterback since the retirement of Dolphins' Hall of Fame quarterback, Dan Marino. To make sure that the young quarterback does succeed, the Dolphins have surrounded the quarterback with young, talented, and strong offensive linemen. In the 2021 N.F.L. draft, the Dolphins added a familiar face to help Tagovailoa become successful with the drafting of his former college teammate from Alabama, wide receiver Jaylen Waddle. Is Tagovailoa the quarterback that the Dolphins have been waiting on for the past 20 plus seasons to catapult the organization as one of the National Football League's premier franchises? My hope is that he is "that quarterback."

Having successful seasons in the N.F.L. are extremely important for a quarterback. In the N.F.L., the quarterback's play can typically tell a lot about an N.F.L, signal caller. According to most N.F.L. insiders and experts, it is during an N.F.L. quarterback's second year that he makes the most improvement.

The Miami Dolphins organization, are no strangers of how a quarterback could significantly improve with experience. Of course, the most recent example of a quarterback making a significant leap in his play is no other than Hall of Fame and Dolphin great, Dan Marino. Marino elevated his play exponentially between his rookie and sophomore seasons.

It was during Marino's second year that he would essentially help the Miami Dolphins become a participant of the Super Bowl, while also shattering passing records. In Dan Marino's second season, he became an N.F.L. legend. I do not have to go into his statistics during his second season because by now most long-time Miami Dolphin fans and historians can still recall his then record breaking season in touchdown passes and passing yards.

As a longtime, devoted, and loyal Dolphins fan, I hope that the search to replace quarterback Dan Marino as the Miami Dolphins undisputed leader at quarterback is finally over. Current quarterback, Tua Tagovailoa has a plethora of pressure that is heavily weighted on his young shoulders. Hopefully, the young signal caller can gain more confidence now that the Dolphins have quarterback whisperer, coach Mike McDaniel. The quarterback has been quoted as saying that "I am thankful that the Miami Dolphins took a chance on me."

Adversity could either make an individual have self-pity, or it could become the fuel for someone to succeed. Tagovailoa has performed outstanding in one of college football's most storied programs. There is a lot of pressure to succeed in a competitive program, such as, the Alabama Crimson Tide.

For Tagovailoa, the stakes to become a successful N.F.L. signal caller for one of the most recognized and successful N.F.L. franchises are significantly higher than it was when he broke into the lineup in the National Championship game as a young 19-year old. If any quarterback other than Dan Marino could potentially resurrect the Dolphins' franchise, it is Tua Tagovailoa. I am interested in seeing how the quarterback will perform for the Miami Dolphins when he continues to gain more valuable experience.

Right now, the left arm of Tagovailoa is one of the ways that the Dolphins could become a force in the A.F.C. East, as well as in the entire National Football League. The young quarterback is a winner. My hope for him is that his health becomes a non-factor in his N.F.L. career.

With another year under his belt, Tagovailoa and the Miami Dolphins have a chance to emerge as one of the National Football League's most young and talented teams. Hopefully, the quarterback will be motivated to prove to many of the critics and experts that he can still become a stellar player in spite of his past adversities due to injury. The Tua Tagovailoa era will hopefully help the Miami Dolphins quest and search to finally replace one of the franchise's most visible quarterbacks.

CHAPTER 6
The Lost Years

Before 2004, the Miami Dolphins only suffered through two losing seasons (1976, 1988), since 1970, which the majority of those years, the late legendary coach, Don Shula was leading the team from the sidelines. There was a plethora of reasons why the Dolphins commenced having losing seasons. The team in 2004 lost 12 games.

As a Dolphin fan, I was not used to the team losing more than seven games within an N.F.L. season. In the two previous seasons before the 2004 N.F.L. campaign, the Dolphins did post winning records of 9 wins in 2002 and 10 wins in 2003, but the team did not qualify for the playoffs. I did not know that beginning in 2004 the Miami Dolphins would struggle to win games in the N.F.L.

From 2004 to 2020, the Miami Dolphins only qualified for the playoffs twice (2008, 2016). This was difficult to get used to. Now I understand that most N.F.L. franchises do suffer from lean years from time to time.

It seems that all the previous years of winning occurred so long ago. A few of the previous Dolphins teams have been able to post winning records, which were the playoff teams in 2008, 2016, 2022, and 2023.

Between 2004 and 2020, the Dolphins would record 10 losing seasons. Of course, these losing seasons did not occur more than three consecutive years. As a fan that has been spoiled by many seasons of winning football played by my beloved Miami Dolphins, it has been both difficult and painful to not see the Dolphins become regular participants in the N.F.L. post-season tournament.

What the Dolphins organization has in its favor is a plethora of rich culture in regard to past history of a winning franchise. High- ranking officials, coaches, and players within the Dolphins organization must not depend on the fact that the Miami Dolphins franchise has been an overall winning organization for many years. When it comes to the Dolphins teams between the years of 2004-2020, I believe that some of those teams really played hard, but at times lacked the mental discipline to not commit errors in a crucial time within a game.

There were some seasons that the Dolphins only had to win just one game to be amongst the playoff teams in that particular season. Some players on the Miami Dolphins had just as much talent as other players in the league, but for whatever reason, their talent could not propel the Dolphins into becoming a perennial playoff team. This is why I believe that the mental aspect of the game is just as vital to a team, than talent alone.

Everyone knows that it requires a special talent just to make an N.F.L. roster. All N.F.L. players have strengths and weaknesses. And the same can be said for the majority of N.F.L. teams.

In my opinion, the Dolphins have been affected by their previous success. The modern N.F.L. does not care about what a team did in the past. Each year must be treated on a yearly basis, because if it is not the season will definitely become lost.

Potential has never won any games in the N.F.L. A team must have players that will put that potential into action. For years I have heard that the Miami Dolphins could be the team to challenge the previous mighty, New England Patriots, and now the. Buffalo Bills, for AFC East supremacy.

Since 2001, the year that the New England Patriots initially won their first of many Super Bowls, the Miami Dolphins have finished in second place in the A.F.C. Eastern division, seven times between 2001 and 2020. This tells me that the Dolphins were not a terrible franchise. They were a franchise that was close, but ultimately not good enough to challenge for the division crown.

It has been frustrating to see all of the consecutive years of success that the New England Patriots enjoyed over the past twenty seasons. Though, the Dolphins would capture the A.F.C. East divisional title in 2008, it pales in comparison to the divisional dominance that the New England Patriots have had all of these years. That team has had a strong grip on the division that sadly the Miami Dolphins have not been successful at stopping or breaking.

As much as it pains me to state this, I will state that unfortunately our divisional rival has been the golden standard of successful teams in the N.F.L. My hope for my beloved Dolphins is that one day, the team and organization can also return to its consistency in winning by regaining momentum by drafting players and signing free agents who have the will to win, instead of collecting a huge paycheck. Think about it.

South Florida is an ideal place to live and play. The weather is primarily tropical all year long and there is not any state income tax. In this region of the country, the beaches, waters, and nightlife can become extremely enticing.

Because of the beauty of Miami, some have unfortunately become lost in the sunshine. Years ago, the city was referred to as a " paradise lost" because of its crime and drug problem in the late 1970s and early 1980s. Miami's professional football team has not been fortunate in having success in winning consistently due to some of the players on previous teams having a complacent attitude and mindset.

Football is a competitive and combat sport. A team that has the desire to win must strive to always go above and beyond the extra mile. I believe in the old saying that hard work really does pay off.

Teams that have a winning culture for a substantial amount of time do not allow losing to remain with them, or become a habitual habit. Over the years, the Miami Dolphins have unfortunately allowed losing to persist. I am cognizant of the fact that many who are loyal and devoted fans of the team do not want to hear that fact.

Sometimes, harsh reality and truth hurts. If one is receptive to what needs to be corrected in order for one to improve, then progress will be made. I wholeheartedly believe that the obstacles and adversities of these lost years for the Miami Dolphins franchise could eventually help the team regain its hunger to win.

Record wise, the 2007 Miami Dolphins was the worst team in team history. The team only had 1 win during the whole entire season. If it were not for a December overtime victory over the Baltimore Ravens, 22 to 16, the Dolphins would have the distinction of being the only franchise to record both a perfect season and a winless season.

I will never forget as a fan how I saw a plethora of fans at the former Dolphin Stadium wearing paper bags over their heads. Immediately, I was reminded of my hometown team, the New Orleans Saints. 2007 was definitely a season to forget.

In my opinion, though the 2007 team was 1-15, I do not believe that the team was amongst the worst teams in N.F.L. history. Most people will only see the 1 win and 15 losses, but as I reflect back on that lost season, the 2007 Miami Dolphins were a competitive one- win football team.

In the N.F.L., I am cognizant of the fact that being competitive is not always viewed in a positive way. When most critics and experts say that a team was competitive, that typically means that the team is losing. Although, the 2007 Miami Dolphins suffered through the worst season in franchise history, I believe that the team was not as bad as its record.

There were six games during that miserable season that the Dolphins lost by three points. This tells me that those games could have gone in the Dolphins' favor. If the Dolphins could have won those six games, they would have finished that 2007 campaign with a total of 7 wins.

Winning 7 games in a N.F.L. season does not also result in a winning record, in 16 games that are played, but it is also respectable. A 7- win season is just 1-win shy away from having an 8 win and 8-loss season. Completing an N.F.L. season at a 500 % winning percentage or better could be considered a season of success.

Also, the 2007 season for the Miami Dolphins would be the first and only season coached by former coach, Cam Cameron. It was also a season of off- the- field distractions. There were multiple arrests of Dolphins players that year.

Former Dolphin linebacker, Joey Porter was involved in an altercation with another N.F.L. player at a casino in Las Vegas. Three other Dolphin players were in the midst of legal troubles when they were arrested in separate incidents. Star Dolphins wide receiver, Chris Chambers rounded out the legal woes for Dolphins players before the start of the 2007 season with a DWI arrest.

These off the field distractions definitely affected that 2007 Miami Dolphins team, due to the team's poor record. Everything that could go wrong in that 2007 campaign did ultimately go wrong. The team's worst- case scenario was on full display in a season, which all Dolphins fans would prefer to block out of their memories.

The 2007 N.F.L. season for the Miami Dolphins will go down as the most unsuccessful season in team history. It is a cautionary tale of how off-the-field distractions could make a negative impact no matter how much optimism that a team has. Hopefully, there will never be a repeat of that dismal 2007 Miami Dolphins campaign.

Top free agents looking for a team to join have avoided joining the Miami Dolphins in recent years. There was a time that top free agents would jump at the chance of signing with the Dolphins. In the 1990s and early 2000s, I can recall how many free agents viewed signing with the Dolphins in Miami as an attractive relocation.

Now, I am not saying that the Dolphins have not signed some notable free agents over the years, but many top of the line free agents have not chosen the Dolphins as a team that they would like to lend their services to. The Miami Dolphins front office has always demonstrated an aggressive approach in regard to free agency.

I believe that when it comes to free agency, the Miami Dolphins front office never exhibited lack of effort in pursuing a player in the free agency market. A notable free agent in recent years that comes to mind that the Dolphins struck out on in free agency is another high-profile free agent quarterback who eventually signed elsewhere. That quarterback with whom I am referring to would be none other than the future Hall of Fame, and former Indianapolis Colt and Denver Bronco, two-time Super Bowl winning quarterback, Peyton Manning.

In 2012, I can recall how the former All-pro quarterback piqued the interest of several teams, including the Miami Dolphins. The city of Miami wanted Manning so badly that there was a huge billboard prominently displayed in the city that showed the talented quarterback in a Miami

Dolphins uniform. Like some who are huge fans of the Miami Dolphins, I was hoping that he would eventually sign with the organization.

It was reported that the quarterback was an admirer of Dolphins Hall of Fame quarterback, Dan Marino when he was a youth. I also heard that Manning was a friend of Marino, after the quarterback became one of the faces of the National Football League. To cap that fact off, it was also reported that Manning owned a home in South Florida. As a Dolphin fan, I thought that those things would influence the former All-world quarterback to eventually become the Miami Dolphins most prized free agent that the team would have ever signed.

Unfortunately, the Dolphins would not become fortunate in signing the most coveted free agent of the 2012 N.F.L. off-season. The quarterback eventually signed a five-year contract with the Denver Broncos. Manning's signing with the team ultimately helped the Broncos capture another Super Bowl trophy when he led the team to victory in Super Bowl 50.

The missed signing of Peyton Manning could also be viewed as another missed opportunity for the Dolphins to land a franchise quarterback since Dan Marino was the team's quarterback in 1999. Through no fault of their own, the Dolphins were not the eventual team that Manning chose to join. Miami was "all in" in acquiring the services of Peyton Manning, but for his own personal reasons, he felt that signing with the Dolphins was not a right fit for him. Maybe the Dolphins roster going into that 2012 season was not as appealing as the team that he would eventually sign with.

Honestly, it pains me to state this fact about my dearly loved Miami Dolphins. But quite frankly the team had been mediocre to less than average for several seasons. Sure, the Dolphins have made the playoffs in recent years, but when the team did make a playoff appearance, immediately, a playoff drought ensues.

Since 2008, when the Dolphins made their first playoff appearance since the 2001 season, the Miami Dolphins have finished two consecutive regular seasons with an overall record of 8-8. That was in the 2013 and 2014 regular seasons. As I recall, the Dolphins in 2013 led the National Football League in the amount of quarterback sacks allowed with 58.

In 2014, it seemed as though it was déjà vu when the Dolphins finished in the same place in the A.F.C. East, which was 3rd, with the same identical 8- win and 8-loss record. According to N.F.L. standards that is a mediocre finish. This was primarily under the Joe Philbin era, the coach who was brought in from the Green Bay Packers.

The former coach of the Miami Dolphins was the offensive coordinator for the Packers. Green Bay would finish in the top ten in offense in the N.F.L, while he was the team's offensive coordinator between 2007-2011. It was due to his expertise on the offensive side of the ball that he helped the franchise win Super Bowl XLV over the Pittsburgh Steelers. When Philbin was hired as the coach of the Miami Dolphins, some thought that he would also be able to help the Dolphins become an offensive talented team.

Unfortunately, Philbin and the Dolphins could not equal the overall team success that the coach had with his former team, the Green Bay Packers. I can recall a past quote from the former Miami Dolphins head coach. He said, " I did not come to the Miami Dolphins just to become mediocre."

The number of seasons the Dolphins suffered through less than mediocre seasons is more than a few. Since 2005, the Miami Dolphins have had at least nine losing seasons. Before the 2004 season, the Miami Dolphins had a total of six losing seasons between 1966-2003.

Statistics do not lie. One of the main reasons why the Miami Dolphins have struggled mightily is due to the team's offensive line play. For many seasons, the offensive line play has been porous overall.

This offensive unit is extremely vital to any team's success. Some naively think that offensive skill players, such as, the wide receiver and running back are the only offensive positions responsible in order for an N.F.L. team to succeed. These positions are important, but a talented offensive line is what makes it possible for the wide receiver to be able to catch the ball downfield.

A quarterback must have time to throw the ball to the receiver. An offensive line that is reliable will allow their signal caller to be upright when trying to complete a pass to the wide receiver. As far as a running back, he needs a talented and solid offensive line to open up running lanes for the running back to gain yardage. Much of the unsuccessful seasons for the Miami Dolphins have commenced with poor offensive line play, which is essentially the "heartbeat" of a team in the N.F.L.

Leadership is extremely vital to the success of a team. A team that has great leadership amongst the players in the locker room will typically have success on the field. In 2013, the Miami Dolphins failed to have adequate leadership within the locker room.

Without getting into the specifics of what occurred during that season, the Miami Dolphins organization were in the midst of the news headlines with the "bullying scandal." Guess where the scandal originated? It commenced when two former Dolphin offensive lineman were at the center of what goes on in many locker rooms in the N.F.L. Now, I do not profess to know all that occurs within an N.F.L. locker room because I never played in the National Football League.

But I have played football in my adolescent years, and I have been in an actual locker room. When I played, locker rooms were loud. Most players in the locker room are joking and horsing around.

It is also in the locker room that most players bond with one another. The 2013 season was not dismal, but once again, the Miami Dolphins organization received negative attention. When a team or organization has inner turmoil, most individuals within the organization, front office members, coaches, players, and equipment managers, would prefer that a grievance be held what is commonly referred to as "in-house."

In-house is a terminology that many who are involved in the day-to-day activities of a sports franchise use to try to settle conflicts, grievances, and turmoil that anyone who is a member of the organization or franchise will not try to solve or settle in public outlets, such as, the news and social medias. As I watched the Miami Dolphins' bullying scandal unfold, I immediately thought to myself about how effective was the leadership. In my opinion, if one of the players had an issue with another player, I would think that the player could go to someone within the locker room who is deemed as the "locker room or clubhouse leader."

Sadly, the player who experienced the "bullying" from his perspective felt alone and ostracized because he did not have anyone that he felt he could talk to or confide in. This is when a leader should have emerged. After viewing the negative headlines that the Dolphins had in the 2013 campaign, I never saw anyone take accountability for what could have been a negative locker room culture.

Also, I believe that the closest teams will play the best with one another on the field when they have cohesiveness off of it. I am not saying that the Dolphins did not have any leaders within the organization, but when it came time for someone within the organization during that time to "step up" I cannot recall if anyone did. The bottom line in my opinion is that consistency in leadership was lacking during that time within the Dolphins organization and franchise in 2013. Though the Miami Dolphins had talent on their active roster, lack of leadership and closeness proved that a team could have a plethora of individual talent, but if the team is lacking in leadership, the team could be lost and not play to its optimum potential.

Briefly, I discussed how the Dolphins could have been victims of their previous success. Most fans have learned that the Miami Dolphins are the only team to have completed an N.F.L. season undefeated, and with a Super Bowl victory at the end of it. When any player who plays for the Miami Dolphins enters into the organization, they are reminded of the undefeated 1972 Miami Dolphins.

There might be a plethora of pressure for an incoming player to live up to the standard that was set by the 1972 team. Now I am only speculating. Of course, I cannot speak for any individual who has worn a Dolphins uniform.

As a fan and football enthusiast, there has to be a sound reason(s) why the Miami Dolphins have underperformed and underachieved over the years. One could blame certain individuals for the team's lack of winning success. Personally, I think that there are several reasons why the Miami Dolphins have been lost as an N.F.L. franchise.

The initial reason why the Dolphins have not had a plethora of team success is lack of continuity from the coaching position. It is difficult to have any kind of consistency in winning when there is a coaching change every couple of years. There were some former coaches that coached for the Dolphins that were not given another opportunity to coach after coaching one dreadful season.

Secondly, another reason why the Dolphins have experienced lack of team success is due to lack of success in picking college players from the draft. Many of the team's draft picks have not panned out. The majority of the players that the Dolphins picked in the draft have either been traded or released at some point.

No team can build on team success without the development of talent from the college ranks. Veterans retire or move on, and any N.F.L. team must have a core of young players who are talented enough to take the place of a veteran starter once he leaves the organization. Young players cannot fully develop and blossom without the help of a reliable coaching staff.

If there is constant turnover in regard to an N.F.L. team's head coaching position, then one cannot expect the team to compete for championships and post-season berths. Each time that a team makes a head coaching change, the head coach has to hire his own staff. Young players who were drafted by the previous coaching regime are at a disadvantage because he might not become the right fit for the new coaching leader, due to each coaching staff's various philosophical approaches to football.

Unfortunately, this puts the young player in a precarious position. He has to either change or adapt his playing technique to the new coaching change, or risk becoming released or traded. Furthermore, the new staff does not have any loyalty or obligation to the players that they inherited because those specific players that was there before the new coaching regime were not picked by them. Lastly, the reason why the Dolphins have not had prolonged success in my opinion, is due to the team's lack of urgency in the playoff push, in December and early January.

Mistakes have been made at all levels of the Miami Dolphins organization in the past. No one who is currently left from those lost years can dispute that known fact. Sometimes mistakes within the Dolphins organization were made repetitively.

For example, the team has drafted and signed veteran players in the past that did not take the winning tradition and culture of the Miami Dolphins seriously. I can recall one particular former player who did not know the divisional opponents of the Miami Dolphins. I believe that when someone is hired on a job, that individual should be aware of the history of the company that they are expected to work for.

Football players, hired by the teams that they sign with, should be cognizant of the team's history and culture. When it comes to an N.F.L. organization that player should at least do research on the organization that they will potentially play for. If an individual is not aware of where the franchise that one is playing for has been in its past, then most likely he will not appreciate the franchise's tradition.

The Miami Dolphins have fallen short of drafting and also signing veterans who have the desire and the will to win consistently. I am not in any way stating that every single draftee or signed veteran never had the desire to win, but with the product that was displayed on the field in previous lost seasons, I am curious about many of those former Dolphin player's mindsets and mentalities. Whether one would like to admit it or not, losing has become widely accepted by some players who previously played for the Miami Dolphins.

I have personally seen some of the younger generation of Dolphins players laughing on the sidelines and at the end of games in which the team might have lost or suffered a lopsided defeat. The message that some of these carefree attitudes of some of the past Dolphin players were sending to all who take the time to see them play is the message that losing is "not a big deal." It was almost as if these players did not care at all about how they played in the game.

Performance is what every N.F.L. team does each Sunday. A team that performs well will in most cases win while teams that perform poorly will suffer defeat. Because the Dolphins organization has been mediocre in the past, one can conclude that the team as a whole has not delivered many past outstanding performances collectively.

Four playoff appearances in the past twenty seasons prove what I have been stating all along in this chapter. Some teams do not have the most talent in the National Football League, but somehow they are able to continue to have a winning culture, despite what other teams around the league are doing. All teams have talent, but what matters in the N.F.L. is how that talent develops and responds to game adversity. The Miami Dolphins winning tradition was lowered when the team's culture of winning was not consistently displayed during the team's weekly performances year after year.

Fan support for the Miami Dolphins franchise has been lacking for many years. As a loyal Dolphins fan, I have seen the crowds at Hard Rock Stadium from a distance. Up until a few seasons ago, I viewed every Dolphin game from my home when I had the Sunday Ticket.

For those who are not familiar with the Sunday Ticket, it was a service provided by a particular cable and satellite company in which an N.F.L. fan can view any game on Sunday, around the National Football League, live. When I had that service, of course, I would tune in to every Dolphin game. I was flabbergasted and shocked that during many of the Dolphin home games there were not many fans supporting the team.

Growing up during the Shula and Marino era, I had grown accustomed to seeing thousands of Dolphin fans filling both the Orange Bowl and what was formerly called, Joe Robbie and Pro Player Stadiums. There were always excited fans during that era that were enjoying the South Florida heat and humidity. It seemed as though Dolphin home games were an exciting event.

As the years have progressed, and the Dolphins have not been quite as successful on the field as they were many years ago, I noticed a gradual decline in home attendance. With the success of the city's college football, basketball, baseball, and ice hockey teams, some fans have elected to give those teams more support. What I have learned the most about professional sports teams and fans is that fans will come out and support a team that is consistently winning.

Professional sports teams in general are supported by fans and sponsors. Most fans and sponsors desire to be amongst a winning franchise and organization. If the team is not successful, then it will affect the fan attendance, as well as the potential of sponsors who would like to become associated with a franchise and organization that wins.

The harsh reality is that most fans and sponsors do not want to be associated with a losing team. Now I am not stating that the Miami Dolphins do not have any fans or sponsors at all because that is not the case. There are some fans and local sponsors of the team that will lend their support no matter what.

We live in a culture and society in which patience and loyalty in many instances are not rewarded. Although, the Miami Dolphins have not been in recent years, a team that is considered amongst the National Football League's most elite teams, on the other hand, the team has not been as dismal as the worst teams that are repetitive losers, year after year. It really saddens me also when I see Dolphins home games on television, and the visiting opponent's teams are filling the stadium.

This is a far cry from the home field advantage that the Miami Dolphins enjoyed a few decades ago. Seeing the lack of support from fans of a franchise and organization that was once considered one of the National Football League's most successful franchises is both sad and bothersome. Loyal and devoted fans of the Miami Dolphins are sometimes outnumbered by fans of the opposing team at home games at Hard Rock Stadium.

Realistically the team has been lost in mediocrity and sub-par seasons, which has significantly affected the team's overall fan support.

Blowout losses are experienced sometimes by some of the most elite teams in the N.F.L. Every team will have a bad outing from time to time. There are some fans that would prefer that their team lose decisively, instead of losing a "nail biter."

In both cases, a loss is a loss no matter how hard one tries to sugarcoat it. I have personally seen the Miami Dolphins lose games in a variety of ways. When the 21st century commenced, I did not know that in the 20th century, the Miami Dolphins would experience its most success.

The Dolphins organization has encountered many adversities in its 50 plus years of operation, but realistically these last 15 or so years have been difficult to bear as a Dolphins fan. Though, I would like to forget all of the lean years that the team has experienced on the field, it still does not affect the amount of love that I had or will have for the original sports franchise in the state of Florida. Personally, these difficult years I believe will make the team and organization better and stronger.

Every sports franchise will not be able to win on a continual basis. That is just a realistic fact. Just like winning can be memorable, losing could also serve as a constant reminder of unwanted memories.

There are some N.F.L. franchises and organizations that have fared far worse than the Miami Dolphins. The Dolphins franchise has experienced a plethora of changes within the organization, as well as on the field. For instance, the team logo and uniforms have transformed a few times.

Under the original Dolphin logo that the team had from 1966-1995, was when the team enjoyed its most success. Now do not get me wrong, there is not anything wrong with the current Dolphin logo, but when I see the original Dolphin logo, immediately it reminds me of the winning consistency and success that the team once enjoyed. Hopefully, those lost years for the Miami Dolphins team could become a thing of the past.

Optimism and patience are required for every Dolphin fan who can still recollect those times when the Dolphins' home stadium was filled with more than 60,000 or more fans cheering for the aqua and orange. My desire and wish is for the Miami Dolphins to return to relevancy and contention for Super Bowl trophies. Winning and success on a consistent basis will erase all of those seasons and years that the Dolphins have struggled on the field.

Fans will soon forget those lean years when the team can finally put together more than two consecutive winning seasons. Does more successful seasons for the Miami Dolphins mean that those lost years are totally behind the team? I hope that it means that the team and organization can create a newfound tradition and winning culture that does not have to necessarily compare with the Dolphins' franchise of yesteryear. Only time will tell if the Miami Dolphins as a team and franchise has turned the corner of a franchise that was once lost, but now could be found back to its rich and winning tradition.

CHAPTER 7
The Bridesmaids of the A.F.C. East

According to Webster's Dictionary, a "bridesmaid" is defined as one that finishes just behind the winner. In the late 1980s and early 1990s, the Miami Dolphins had to contend with the Buffalo Bills. Those Bills teams of that era were a force in the A.F.C, as well as in the A.F.C. East.

It was frustrating for me as a loyal Dolphins fan to experience my team falling to the divisional rival Bills. The rivalry between the Dolphins and the Bills were the most intense when Dan Marino and Jim Kelly were quarterbacks for their respective teams. I was cognizant of the fact that the Bills franchise, as well as its fans really loathed the Miami Dolphins.

In the 1970s and early 1980s, the Dolphins ruled the A.F.C. Eastern division. Though, the Dolphins lost two Super Bowls in the decade of the 1980s, they were typically the team in the A.F.C. that other A.F.C. opponents had to defeat in order to have a chance to compete in the A.F.C. Playoffs and Championship games. Buffalo was not at all considered a team to beat in the A.F.C. East prior to the arrival of former Kansas City Chiefs and Buffalo Bills head coach, Hall of Fame inductee, Marv Levy.

In the mid to late 1980s, the Bills were gradually becoming better as a team and franchise. The Bills landed Hall of Fame quarterback, Jim Kelly initially. Next, they commenced to draft players in the N.F.L. college draft who could challenge the divisional rival, Dolphins within the division. The drafting of Hall of Fame players, such as, Hall of Fame defensive end, Bruce Smith, and Hall of Fame wide receiver, Andre Reed, in 1985 would be the team's defensive and offensive cornerstones for the next several seasons.

From 1988 to 1991, the Buffalo Bills were all alone at the top of the A.F.C. East, and would become participants of four consecutive Super Bowls, all of which they lost. It was during those years that the Miami Dolphins would be in an unfamiliar role. That role was looking up at the "little brother" Buffalo Bills, a team that they dominated for an entire decade.

When the Buffalo Bills were finally a team on the rise, it was unfamiliar and uncharted territory for the Miami Dolphins. For many seasons, the Buffalo Bills were the Miami Dolphins' "punching bags." After the team learned how to draft and put together talented players who could compete with the likes of A.F.C. Teams, such as, the Miami Dolphins, for approximately six N.F.L. seasons, the Buffalo Bills never looked back.

They (the Buffalo Bills) were finally the talk of the A.F.C., as well as the whole entire National Football League. In many of the Bills' Super Bowl runs, the road to the ultimate game had to go through them. So, if an A.F.C. playoff opponent wanted to become a participant in the Super Bowl, the opponent had to win in the winter climate of Buffalo, New York.

There was a 1990 playoff game between the Buffalo Bills and my Miami Dolphins in which I learned just how much of a competitive advantage that playing in the snow would become for the hometown Bills. This game was a shoot-out. I realized during that game how difficult it would become for the Dolphins to win against a team that they once dominated.

Rain and snow would become a dominant factor in this particular playoff match up. For the visiting Dolphins, they played extremely well given the circumstances in regard to the weather. It was a game that would favor both offenses, and hurt both team's defensive units.

As I reflect back on that game, the game was ultimately lost in the first quarter by the Miami Dolphins. The reason why I am stating that fact is because both teams scored the identical amount of points from the second quarter through the fourth quarter. In the first quarter, the Bills grabbed a 10- point lead.

34 to 44 would become the final score of that game, which was held in frigid Orchard Park, New York. I can recall thinking how the Dolphins were not able to slow down Kelly and his high-powered offense in the rain and snow. Although, the Dolphins split both meetings with the Bills in that 1990 regular season campaign, they still finished in second place that year behind the Kelly led Bills.

This game helped propel the Bills into A.F.C. dominance and supremacy. Miami was good enough that year to compete with the Bills, but essentially not good enough to capture the A.F.C. East crown, nor a playoff victory over the Bills. During that 1990 season, I can still recall how many of the announcers were talking about how the Dolphins' defense had to improve in order for the team to challenge for a playoff berth.

Most of that season, the Dolphins defense played hard-nosed and inspired football. Miami's defense only gave up more than 24 points during a game once all year. Statistically, in points allowed, the Dolphins finished first in the division by allowing a total of 242 points all season.

After watching that dramatic playoff win versus the Kansas City Chiefs, when former Dolphins great, wide receiver, Mark Clayton scored a 12-yard touchdown with 2:28 left in regulation, in a 17 to 16 victory, I remember thinking that the defense finally matched the team's explosive talent on offense. To my surprise, during that playoff contest in the snow against the divisional rival, Buffalo Bills, I did not envision that the Dolphins' defense would give up the most points (44) that it had surrendered all season to a divisional foe that I thought that the Dolphins matched up well with.

In my opinion, the Dolphins' offense did its part by scoring 34 points. That was quite an accomplishment considering how difficult it is for any team to play in unfavorable weather conditions. Also, I can recall thinking about what could have been.

Early in the 1990 season in week 2, the Miami Dolphins played an inspired regular season game when they blew out the divisional rival, Buffalo Bills, 30 to 7, in Miami. I thought that the win set the tone for how well the Dolphins would play for the majority of games they would play that year. Although, the Bills would seek revenge in the week 16 match up when they won 24 to 14 over the Dolphins, I still held hope that the Dolphins would become victorious in the snow in both team's playoff match. Because the Bills won the tie-breaking "rubber match" game in the 1990 post-season, the Dolphins would again have to settle in becoming "second fiddle" to the rival Bills.

Enduring the Buffalo Bills' dominance in the late 1980s and early 1990s was definitely a "hard pill" to swallow. The coaching matchup between legendary coaches, Don Shula and Marv Levy did not fare well for Shula. After dominating that one particular franchise with a 29-3 overall coaching record versus the Bills through the 1985 regular season, when Levy became the head coach in 1986, Shula and the Dolphins' success over the Buffalo Bills commenced to turn in the Bills' favor.

1986 would be the last year that the Dolphins would sweep a Bills team in the Shula led era with the Dolphins. When the Buffalo Bills became a dominant team in the A.F.

C. East, as well as in the A.F.C., I must say that I did not expect it. In 1985 and 1986, the Bills ended those years with double- digit losses.

During the 1987 N.F.L. strike-shortened season, the Bills once again had a losing record, but any N.F.L. observer could tell that the team had significantly improved. One way that the 1987 season signaled improvement for the Buffalo Bills is how competitive they were. The team beat the reigning Super Bowl champion, New York Giants in a hard fought defensive battle, 6 to 3, although every team would play much of the 1987 season with replacement players.

These players were just that, replacements. They filled in for the regular players on what was then a league, which consisted of a total of 28 N.F.L. teams. Some regular N.F.L. veterans played with the replacement players due to obligation to receive a regular N.F.L. paycheck.

Many of these men would have liked to stand in solidarity with the majority of N.F.L. veterans who were on strike for legitimate reasons and concerns. But N.F.L. veterans who made the minimum in player's salary could not afford to remain in the N.F.L. Player's Union picket lines for long.

Some players had families to take care of, as well as mouths to feed. Whether the Bills and Dolphins along with the 26 other N.F.L. franchises played replacement games with replacement players or not, the games that were played during that season counted the same way in which it always did. The Bills avenged and atoned for their previous two- game sweep by the Miami Dolphins in the previous season with a sweep of their own doing.

Buffalo would win a close game in Miami with a 34 to 31 victory over my beloved Dolphins in a hostile home crowd of over 61,000. Several weeks later in week 11, the Bills would then win in convincing fashion with a 27-0 thumping over the Dolphins. This particular defeat captured my attention.

The late great coach of the Miami Dolphins, Don Shula probably also noticed how the Buffalo Bills had improved from A.F.C. East doormat, to a team that would be on the rise in the future. Buffalo had plenty of incentive to "take it to" my Dolphins. Years of frustration culminated in that last regular season shutout against the team that was the Bills' unbeatable nemesis and foe for so long.

Marv Levy and Jim Kelly have received the most credit for the Bills' A.F.C. East and A.F.C. Conference dominance for those approximately six years of A.F.C reign. There were other men in that franchise during those years of A.F.C. dominance that are not credited enough. Hall of Fame defensive end, Bruce Smith was a dominant defensive end, and it seemed like he played his best games against Marino and the Dolphins.

His fellow defensive teammates, linebackers Cornelius Bennett and Darryl Talley also were formidable defensive foes. On offense, Hall of Fame quarterback Jim Kelly, Hall of Fame running back, Thurman Thomas, and Hall of Fame wide out, Andre Reed were definitely "thorns in the side" of the Miami Dolphins. Also, I cannot forget the Bills' special team's standouts, gunner Steve Tasker and kick return specialist, Don Beebe who also seemed to play their best games against their divisional rival from South Florida.

All of these players that I just mentioned all had a hand in stopping the Dolphins from regaining dominance in the A.F.C. East, as well as the entire A.F.C. Conference in the latter part of the 1980s and early to mid-1990s.

Karma was not on the side of the Dolphins during that span. The Dolphins had to take a heavy dose of "humble pie" when they were not able to succeed in winning a plethora of games against the now divisional rivals. Before the Bills improvement prior to the 1987 season, the Buffalo Bills versus the Miami Dolphins rivalry was non-existent.

A rivalry that is worth viewing on television on Sunday is typically not one-sided. Great rivalries in sports, and in particular in the N.F.L. are competitive. Most rivalry games that are interesting are between teams that do not have dominance over the other.

In the late 1980s and early 1990s, Bills and Dolphins fans were not bored. Though, the Bills would win most of the match ups during that span, I must say that as a fan and Miami Dolphins enthusiast, many of those games were entertaining and came down to the last quarter. There was a plethora of regular season games in the Levy and Kelly led era for the Buffalo Bills that left my heart broken during that span

I can recall one memorable Bills/Dolphins game in which quarterback Jim Kelly won the game in the waning seconds with a scramble up the middle of the Dolphins defense. It was after that last-second victory that I knew that the Buffalo Bills were for real. Although, I will never become a fan of the Buffalo Bills, I gained respect for their "never say die" mentality and relentless pursuit of victory when Marv levy was the head coach and Jim Kelly was the team's signal caller.

These same Buffalo Bills would once again unceremoniously send coach Shula into retirement. In the 1995 Wild Card playoffs, the Miami Dolphins would face a familiar divisional foe in the Buffalo Bills. Just like the playoff match up in the 1990 post-season, the Dolphins would have to travel in the inclement weather. I can still recall how the game was played on a Saturday. After going to the donut shop to get donuts, I was anticipating an exciting game, but the game would not be as advertised, with the Dolphins being shutout in the first three quarters, until they scored a barrage of points (22) in the game's final period. Sadly, the Dolphins could not overcome the A.F.C. East dominance that the Bills enjoyed, while coach Shula was patrolling the sidelines in the final years of his outstanding coaching career.

Once Shula retired, which was a week after that uneventful playoff game against the Buffalo Bills, another coach was hired to replace the legendary coach. The Dolphins would replace coach Shula with Hall of Fame coach, Jimmy Johnson. Johnson experienced an enormous amount of success when he was the coach of his former team, the Dallas Cowboys.

Coach Johnson resurrected a floundering Dallas Cowboys franchise when he would win two consecutive Super Bowls with that storied organization. It was due to Johnson's influence on the N.F.L. draft that the Dallas Cowboys became restored to glory in the early to mid-1990s. Ironically, the two Super Bowl victories that Johnson won were against the Dolphins' familiar divisional foe, the Buffalo Bills.

Johnson led the Cowboys to victory in Super Bowls XXVII and XXVIII in 1992 and 1993. There was hope that the Dolphins would eventually overcome the Buffalo Bills' reign of supremacy in the A.F.C East. The Dolphins hire of coach Jimmy Johnson was not only made to help propel the Dolphins into contention for Super Bowls, but the hiring of the talented coach and evaluator was made to overtake the hated team from Western New York.

In Johnson's first season with the Dolphins, the goal and mission to defeat those detested Buffalo Bills was accomplished. Although, Miami would finish a game below their 1995 regular season's record at 8-8, the Dolphins did something that was not done since 1986. Johnson and the Dolphins would enjoy a season sweep of the team that had tormented the Dolphins for the past nine seasons.

The first meeting between the Bills and Dolphins in the 1996 N.F.L regular season was an atonement game. Miami won that revenge game by a score of 21 to 7 in Buffalo. That win was satisfying for the Dolphins because in recent years it had been difficult for the Dolphins to come away with a victory in Buffalo.

Week 16 of the 1996 regular season would also have the same result for the Miami Dolphins. On a Monday night in Miami, with a home crowd of a little over 67,000, the Dolphins continued their winning ways over the divisional foe, Buffalo Bills with a 16 to 14 victory. For many Dolphin fans, the 1996 season sweep over the Buffalo Bills who would eventually be in the N.F.L. post-season that year was extremely gratifying.

After the 1996 season, the Buffalo Bills would only make the playoffs twice before the 2017 N.F.L. season. One of those playoff games the Bills would play was against the hated Dolphins in the 1998 Wild Card playoffs. For several years, the Buffalo Bills had the "upper hand" on the Miami Dolphins.

On that day in early January of 1999 at the formerly named Pro Player Stadium in Miami, the Dolphins would finally claim a playoff revenge victory over the Bills. It was the Dolphins' defense that was the aggressor during that 24 to 17 Dolphins win, when they were able to force five Bills turnovers. I can recall thinking that the Dolphins finally "exercised the demons" when they were no longer a bridesmaid to that hated divisional rival.

1996 was the first of many seasons that the Dolphins would have to contend with another A.F.C. East team that would eventually take the whole N.F.L. by storm. During the 1997 season, the Bills and Dolphins would split the season series. It was not just the Buffalo Bills that would draw concern for many Dolphin fans.

It was another divisional opponent that would soon rise above every team in the A.F.C. East, including the Dolphins. The team with whom I am referring to is none other than the New England Patriots. By 1997, the Buffalo Bills would no longer have a tight reign on both the A.F.C. East, as well as the entire American Football Conference.

New England also came out of nowhere to challenge and win the A.F.C. Eastern divisional title in 1996. Just a season before in 1995, the New England Patriots finished the season almost at the bottom of the A.F.C East standings with a 6-win and 10-loss overall record. The team from the upper Northeast went from a team almost at the bottom of the division to a team that would claim the A.F.C. title over both the Buffalo Bills and the Miami Dolphins.

For several years in the late 1980s up until the mid-1990s, the A.F.C. East went through Buffalo. The Miami Dolphins seemed like the team in that division who would most likely pose a challenge. Finally, when the Dolphins did pose a challenge to the Buffalo Bills, their dominance over the A.F.C. East would be over.

With the retirements of coach Marv Levy and quarterback Jim Kelly, the Buffalo Bills would no longer pose a real threat to every divisional opponent that the team once dominated in the A.F.C. East. In 1997, the Dolphins improved one game in the win column from the previous season in 1996, which was coach Jimmy Johnson's first season as the Miami Dolphins head coach. The 1997 season was a positive season for the Dolphins because the team would return to the N.F.L. post-season, after a year-long absence from the N.F.L. playoff tournament.

Although, a playoff berth was a positive occurrence for the 1997 Miami Dolphins, the season would also become filled with negative occurrences on the field, which was courtesy of the New England Patriots. During the 1997 regular season, the Patriots would sweep the Dolphins by defeating them in two close contests. Also, the Patriots defeated the Dolphins in the regular season finale that year.

To make matters worse, the Dolphins would have to face this new nemesis again in the Wild Card playoffs the very next week. I still can recall thinking to myself leading up to that game that it is difficult to defeat any team in sports three times in the same season. As a football fan, I never recalled a football team winning triple times, over the same opponent, let alone an opponent from the same division.

Though, the Dolphins finished in second place that season to the then-upstart, Patriots, the third and final game that both teams would play that year, resulted in a dismal 17 to 3, Miami Dolphins defeat. After viewing that lackluster performance, I was on high alert again for another A.F.C. East opponent that the Dolphins would soon again play second runner up to. That defeat in New England would serve as the catalyst of what was to come in the A.F.C. East in the future.

Fast forward to 2001, the Miami Dolphins and the New England Patriots would have a photo finish en route to the A.F.C. Eastern divisional crown. That season, both teams split the regular season meetings between one another. Also, the two teams would also finish the season with the same won/loss record of 11 wins and 5 defeats.

Unfortunately, for the Miami Dolphins they lost the division that year due to the Patriots better point differential. So, yet again, the Dolphins would finish the regular season just behind the eventual Super Bowl victor. When the Dolphins was bounced in the playoffs 20 to 3, by the incumbent Super Bowl champion, Baltimore Ravens, I can vividly remember thinking that the Ravens could repeat again because they again had a dominant defense.

During that 2001-02 post- season, the Dolphins were a 4th seed, while the Patriots were a 2nd seed. In that playoff format, 3-through 6th seeds had to play in the Wild Card games the week before the higher seeds, the 1st and 2nd seeds were fortunate to have the week off. A 1st and 2nd seed always has a competitive advantage.

First, the 1st and 2nd seeds in each conference will have an extra week of rest. Also, the higher seeds were able to prepare for the opponent that they will face in the divisional round.

Lastly, the former playoff format made it easier for the higher seed to reach the Conference championship.

If the Dolphins were able to get the number 2 seed, they would have already advanced to the divisional round of the playoffs. The road to the Super Bowl might have been in clear view. Of course, I am stating this scenario hypothetically. What I am really trying to say is that the Dolphins' second place finish was the difference between the Dolphins advancing and resting in the playoff tournament.

It was in the 2001 playoffs, that the New England Patriots established themselves as a team of destiny. The Patriots were a perennial playoff team, but no one could have predicted that they would (1) win their first of many Super Bowls (2) upset a talented Rams squad (3) and lastly, become a dynasty that would last for approximately twenty consecutive seasons. For the Miami Dolphins, on the other hand, the Patriots surge into not only A.F.C. supremacy, but N.F.L. dominance, meant that the team from South Florida would have to endure another team from the A.F.C. East that would become a mainstay in the N.F.L. spotlight.

New England became the new "big brother" in the A.F.C. East. Out of all of the teams in the A.F.C. East that have enjoyed the most success in playing the New England Patriots, I believe that the Miami Dolphins have been the team in that division that has challenged the Patriots the most. Just because the Dolphins have been formidable opponents to the powerhouse Patriots should not make the Dolphins franchise and organization feel any better.

Year after year, up until the 2020 N.F.L. season, the Patriots would win the A.F.C. East an unprecedented 17 out of 20 possible seasons. This feat might never be experienced by any other N.F.L. franchise again. In the midst of the Patriots success, the Dolphins have usually been the Patriots' runner-up in the division that they (the Patriots) have basically owned.

Dominant teams and eras in the A.F.C. East have affected the Miami Dolphins' quest to become a front-runner in the A.F.C. Eastern division. Since 2008, the franchise has only won the division title once. Currently, the Buffalo Bills are the team in the A.F.C. East that the rest of the division must to strive to conquer.

The Buffalo Bills and New England Patriots have taken turns in dominating the A.F.C. East. When the Dolphins were a perennial playoff team in the early to late 1990s, much of those years were spent trying to overtake Buffalo. In the early 2000s up until Tom Brady's departure, the Dolphins have been forced to deal with all of those seasons of Patriot success.

As a devoted Dolphins fan, I have seen the franchise's frustration with always having to finish second to these teams. After those nine years of Bills dominance, then the Patriots grip on the A.F.C. East ensued. I believe many Dolphin fans would forego finishing second in the division for a chance to make another playoff run deep into the A.F.C. playoffs, then ultimately the Super Bowl.

Finishing multiple seasons in second place is not fatal. It could be worse. Although, the Miami Dolphins in the past 25 or so years have had to encounter two powerhouse teams within their own division does not mean that the Dolphins should accept many of their second place finishes as the norm.

The Dolphins should aim high. There is a solid foundation that the Miami Dolphins have in order to propel themselves from a perennial second place team that is considered the "bridesmaids" to a team and franchise of greatness. One positive way of viewing the Dolphins' plethora of runner-up finishes is that the franchise is not a bad one.

Another positive perception of a second place finish is that when a team is in second place, that team does not have far to go to win. Fortunately, for the Dolphins, the current team is young and talented, and potentially primed for success. Dolphin fans, as well as the Dolphins franchise itself have been waiting for the team to resurge into future glory, and ultimately distance itself from all of its plethora of second place finishes.

In a thirty- year span, the Dolphins have endured two A.F.C. East teams that would make it to a combined 14 Super Bowl appearances. Buffalo's four straight appearances in the Super Bowl in the early 1990s set the tone for teams in the A.F.C East who were head and shoulders above the rest. The New England Patriots, though I do not like to admit it, have been the "cream of the crop" in the A.F.C. Eastern division, as well as in the American Football Conference for so long that their winning culture and success has outlasted several terms of U.S. Presidents.

Sadly, for Dolphins fans, the Patriots have leapfrogged over the Dolphins as the most successful team in the A.F.C. East. Personally, I do not like the fact that the Patriots organization is responsible for yet another second place finish. What I am referring to is the number of overall franchise wins. The Patriots are first in the division in overall wins that is to date 541 wins. The Dolphins are of course second in overall franchise wins all-time with a win total of 496 victories.

Can the Dolphins emerge from being the second place finisher to powerful teams in the A.F.C. East? I believe that anything is possible. In the 2020 N.F.L. season, the Dolphins improved drastically. The season before, the Dolphins were a young team that was just trying to find its way.

Miami improved from 5 wins, to a 10-win team in just one full season. They also finished the 2020, 2021,2022, 2023 regular seasons in a familiar place. You guessed it.

It was another second place finish for the Miami Dolphins. This time the Dolphins did not finish the season behind familiar A.F.C. East front-runner, the New England Patriots. New England had an uncharacteristic down year.

From 2020 to 2023, the division champion in the A.F.C. East was the Buffalo Bills. Buffalo also has a core of talented players, like the Dolphins.

As a Dolphin fan, I have seen this movie. The Buffalo Bills positioning themselves for another A.F.C. Eastern division take over. For approximately a decade and a half, the Buffalo Bills have not been as successful as a franchise as they were in the decade of the 1990s. The team had endured a plethora of years of struggle, as well.

Now, the Bills are poised to make a run not only as a force in the A.F.C. East, but Buffalo could also emerge as a powerhouse team in the whole entire American Football Conference. New England, on the other hand, was a team in transition in the 2020 season. Long-time, and future Hall of Fame quarterback of the Patriots, Tom Brady, elected to take his talent to the Tampa Bay Buccaneers.

With Brady and Coach Belichick's departures from the Patriots, the team is in unfamiliar territory.

Miami and Buffalo have both become talented teams. I am curious about how the Dolphins will fare in the upcoming 2024 season. No one can say that the A.F.C. East is not competitive.

Personally, I expect each team from the A.F.C. East to improve. Maybe the New York Jets will also be in the mix in the competitive balance in the A.F.C. East. For the Dolphins, I hope that they could somehow overcome the emergence of the young and confident Buffalo Bills.

The Dolphins have enough young talent on the field and on the coaching staff to challenge all of the other teams within their division. They (the Dolphins) made the playoffs in 2022 for the first time since 2016. Also, the Dolphins made a playoff run in the 2023 season, although it was short-lived. What team stood in the way of the Dolphins being able to succeed in the 2022 playoff tournament? It was of course the hated Buffalo Bills that beat the Dolphins in a narrow playoff victory in Buffalo. Miami entered the contest with their third-stringed quarterback, Skylar Thompson, after the season-ending concussion injury to starter, Tua Tagovailoa. The Dolphins barely lost by a score of 31 to 34. Miami should have plenty of motivation to win versus both the Buffalo Bills and the New England Patriots in the ensuing years.

In the 2023 season, the Miami Dolphins had a season-long lead in the A.F.C. East. By season's end, the Dolphins would eventually relinquish the lead in the division by losing a must-win game for the division, 21-14 in Miami. The Dolphins went from being the #2 seed to the #6 seed. Because the Dolphins lost the division, the team had to go on the road to frigid Kansas City and play the Chiefs, which led to a lopsided loss, 26-7.

They say that bridesmaids cannot become bridesmaids forever. My hope is that in the Miami Dolphins' case, that particular saying proves true. The Dolphins are due for a dominant run in the A.F.C. East.

There have been many years and seasons that the Dolphins have endured two A.F.C. East divisional rival dynasties. Miami has always been the challenger, but not the conqueror, when those A.F.C. East teams became dominant in the league. The Dolphins have to figure out how to defeat those teams within their division when it counts.

As a Dolphin fan, the truth hurts. Realistically, the team has not showed up in games against these dynasties in which they had to win. I believe that the Dolphins always had enough physical talent to win those big games against their divisional foes, but for whatever reason, the team has lacked consistency in winning.

Just like I previously stated, all N.F.L. teams have talent. In life, the most talented and intelligent individual is not the most successful person. Many factors could contribute to an individual who has all the talent and intelligence to succeed, but the most vital determinant of any individual's success is that individual's attitude and overall mental makeup.

Teams are responsible for each N.F.L. organization's success. Football is best played when the team as a whole can hold each individual accountable. It is also the attitude and mentality of the team, which could be the difference between continuous and sporadic success.

Motivation to win is key to winning for a prolonged time. The Miami Dolphins should have plenty of motivation when it comes to winning because of the success of their other divisional rivals. Miami has not won an A.F.C. Championship since the 1984 N.F.L. season. All of the other teams in the A.F.C. East have reached the A.F.C. Championship at least twice within the last 15 years.

Even the struggling New York Jets have reached the A.F.C. Championship more times than the Miami Dolphins have within the last 20 seasons. Although, the Buffalo Bills have not reached an A.F.C. Championship since the early 1990s, at least they had a chance to play in the Super Bowl, which is also a feat that the Dolphins have not enjoyed for over thirty-plus years. The Dolphins should not only be pleased with just making the playoffs, they should be hungry for more.

The team and organization cannot rely upon the success of yesteryear. That was in the past, which cannot be changed. A team can always alter or change their current mentality and attitude with winning football games.

The Miami Dolphins are due to having a dynasty themselves. They should channel all their seasons and years of being the division runner ups to divisional and N.F.L. dynasties into motivation to create their own longevity in winning. One day, hopefully the "bridesmaids" of the A.F.C. East will ascend into divisional, as well as N.F.L. dominance again.

CHAPTER 8
Dolphins New Era

Innovative, is a word to describe the Dolphins organization these days. The reason why I can state that the franchise is innovative does not come from my own bias. There are three important positions that each N.F.L. team has.

A reliable general manager is the first of those important positions that is extremely vital to an N.F.L. organization. Besides the team's owner and president, the general manager is responsible for shaping up the roster. He is in charge of picking the college talent, as well as the N.F.L. veterans who are the best fits for the team.

General manager, Chris Grier, who happens to be an African-American is one of the few minority general managers in the entire N.F.L. Grier has held the position since 2016. In his first season at that important position, he made bold moves by trading the 8th overall pick for the rights to draft highly touted left tackle, Laremy Tunsil, who slid to the Dolphins at the number 13th overall pick position, after a controversial video of him surfaced. With his input on the roster, Grier's reworking of the Dolphin's roster helped the Dolphins earn their first playoff berth in approximately seven seasons.

Grier is not afraid to make aggressive moves. When a former Dolphins head coach was not getting the most out of his team, Grier pulled the trigger and dismissed the once highly sought after coach, Adam Gase, after three years at the helm in 2018. Before the start of the 2019 N.F.L. regular season, Grier made another surprising and aggressive move by trading talented Pro-Bowl offensive tackle, Laramy Tunsil to the Houston Texans for two first round picks and a second-round pick. Also, a few years later, the general manager parted ways with an underachieving former first round quarterback, Ryan Tannehill.

In the 2020 draft, Grier took a chance on former Alabama quarterback, Tua Tagovailoa, who suffered a devastating hip injury, which caused him to slide from potentially becoming the first overall pick in the draft to that year's 5th selection of the Miami Dolphins. The general manager's aggressive and bold style was also displayed in a 3-team blockbuster trade involving the San Francisco 49ers and Philadelphia Eagles' first round draft picks.

First he traded the 3rd overall pick that the Dolphins held to the 49ers in exchange for their pick. Then, Grier made a trade with the Philadelphia Eagles who owned the 6th pick. Those aggressive trades by general manager, Chris Grier has been responsible for the Dolphins accumulating young college prospects.

Another important position in the N.F.L. is the head coaching position. Grier hired talented head coach, Mike McDaniel as the Dolphins head coach. Thus far, the hiring of McDaniel has proved to be a great hire.

Since coach McDaniel has been the head coach of the Miami Dolphins, the team has developed into an offensive juggernaut. Earlier, I stated that the Dolphins are innovative. In my opinion, the team is definitely innovative by having the most important positions in the team's franchise, held by three minority men. General manager, Chris Grier, who is African-American, head coach, Mike McDaniel, who is of partly African-American, and quarterback Tua Tagovailoa, who is of Hawaiian descent.

Rising from a team of chaos, to a team of respectability is what the Dolphins have accomplished in a few short seasons. I can recall a time when the Dolphins were a dreadful team. In the first seven games of the Flores era, it looked as though the Dolphins would be trending in a negative trajectory.

Although, the Flores era for the Miami Dolphins was short-lived, the Dolphins seemed to be on the cusp of becoming a real contender. Under the direction of Flores, the team gained a reputation of being one that was hard-nosed. In other words, the defense was the heart and soul of the Dolphins during Flores' tenure.

In a surprising move after the 2021 season and season sweep of divisional rival, New England Patriots, the Miami Dolphins parted ways with Coach Flores after three seasons. His teams reflected his no-nonsense style of coaching. It seemed as though he and his Dolphins teams were just a play or game away from reaching the post-season tournament.

On February 6, 2022, the Miami Dolphins hired a young, talented, coach who had previously been the assistant coach of the 49ers under 49ers Head Coach Kyle Shanahan. Head Coach Mike McDaniel became the fourteenth coach of the Miami Dolphins franchise. I must say that the hire has thus far proven to be a very solid hire.

With the hire of McDaniel, the philosophy and identity of the Dolphins has changed dramatically. Under Coach Flores, the Miami Dolphins were primarily known as a defensive-oriented team. The team played with grit and griminess under former head coach, Flores. Playing with that mentality was fine, but realistically, that style of play did not equate to perennial playoff berths.

Coach Mike McDaniel's coaching style is extremely different than the former Dolphin coaching regime. He (Coach McDaniel) is known for orchestrating and designing offensive schemes that are exciting and fun for the average fan. Under the new coaching regime, the Miami Dolphins have become well known throughout the N.F.L. for their explosive offensive play. McDaniel has brought back a brand of football that as a fan, I have been longing for since the days of Marino, Duper, and Clayton.

On offense, the Dolphins have assembled an offensive unit that has finally provoked fear in defenses around the league. For the last several seasons, General Manager Chris Greer has accumulated players who are basically track stars, who happen to play football very well. Tyreek Hill and Jaylen Waddle have become known as the "Splash Brothers". These talented wide receivers have become N.F.L. superstars with their speed and reliable hands. The talented duo has only played two seasons with one another, and when Tyreek Hill was traded to the Miami Dolphins from the mighty Kansas City Chiefs in the 2022 off-season, his addition brought hope and excitement back to an organization that was greatly in need of a boost. If the Dolphins can continue to improve and build upon their playoff berths of 2022 and 2023, then consistency and success could soon ensue. These young talented Dolphins players could help the team continue to be amongst the teams in the N.F.L. on the rise. In addition, to talented wide receivers, Hill and Waddle, the Dolphins have also built balance on offense with speedy and talented running backs, Raheem Mostert and De'Von Achane.

The Miami Dolphins in 2023 have become an exciting team to watch. It is extremely refreshing to see that the Miami Dolphins are currently a well-balanced team, especially on offense. This current Dolphin team is balanced with a potent running attack and passing offense that could rival any explosive offense in N.F.L. history.

In 2023, the Dolphins surprised a plethora of fans and critics with an explosive and talented offense. After starting the 2020 campaign with 1 win and 3 losses, the Dolphins won 9 out of 12 games. Due to the team's strong finish, they were in the midst of the playoff hunt. This was the catalyst of hope and the start of the Dolphins becoming potential winners.

Although, the Dolphins ultimately did not make the playoffs in the end, the team from South Florida had many of positive moments. There is a strong mental toughness that I sensed from these new members of the Miami Dolphins. It seemed that in previous seasons when the Dolphins got off to a slow start, the team could not climb out of its predicament.

For many seasons, the Miami Dolphins would start slow and then remain there for the rest of the season. The Dolphins are a young team. I believe that when many of the first and second year players were thrown into the fire by being forced to play, that essentially helped the young Dolphins to become mentally tough.

Miami's defense has the potential of becoming a force to be reckoned with. With the combination of young talent and veterans, the Dolphins defense has the potential of becoming one of the National Football League's elite. Though, I personally love offensive football, I really became intrigued by the play of the defense.

I love the way that the defense swarms around the ball. Many years ago, at the tail end of the Shula era, the Dolphins defense was considered "soft" or in other words, "pushovers." When Jimmy Johnson was the coach of the Dolphins, he tried to change the Dolphins' whole mentality on defense. The team under Shula, for most of quarterback Dan Marino's career were primarily known as an offensive passing team.

Most teams that played the Dolphins when Marino, Duper, and Clayton were lighting it up on the scoreboard knew that if they stopped the talented trio, Miami's defense would not be able to stop the opposing offense on a consistent basis. After coach Jimmy Johnson retired after the 1999 season, the Dolphins have been struggling to identify their own mentality as a team. Under the previous coaches who have coached the Miami Dolphins after coach Dave Wannstedt, who was Jimmy Johnson's successor, the Dolphins were not a team of either a strong offensive or defensive identity.

As of now, I envision the Miami Dolphins becoming more of a balanced team. Right now, the offensive side of the ball is the team's strength, but with the steady progression of the talent on defense, the defensive unit could also become a force. The current Miami Dolphins team, that are headed by head coach, Mike McDaniel, could have their most balanced team, since coach Don Shula's teams helped turn the Dolphins into a Super Bowl champion many seasons ago.

Coach Mike McDaniel is a coach that the Miami Dolphins definitely need. He was an assistant under Coach Kyle Shanahan (current San Francisco 49ers coach), whose father Mike Shanahan was a brilliant coach and Super Bowl winning coach of the Denver Broncos. The elder Shanahan's teams were known for their balance on offense.

Of course, many are aware of the success of the San Francisco 49ers and Denver Broncos. Their winning culture and tradition over the years have been undeniable. I must admit that I wish the Dolphins would one day enjoy the success that those teams have encountered.

Coach McDaniel comes from the Shanahan coaching tree. He also had stops in Houston and Washington, before he became the current head coach of the Miami Dolphins. Although, I heard little about him prior to his hire as Dolphins head man, I must admit that he has influenced the Miami Dolphins current team culture.

McDaniel has brought his winning formula to the Miami Dolphins who have been in need of a winning culture for a plethora of years. Initially, his tenure with the Dolphins got off to a surprisingly great start.

In the Dolphins' first eight games of the 2022 N.F.L. season, he led the Dolphins to a 5-3 record. His first two games as a head coach came against the then mighty and former head coach of the New England Patriots Bill Belichick, and his second game as a Dolphins coach was against Coach John Harbaugh, who is an elite coach within his own right. Coach McDaniel beat both coaches. Soon, the N.F.L. had to take notice.

Prior to Coach McDaniel's arrival, the Dolphins were on the cusp of being a playoff-caliber team. I credit McDaniel and his staff as being one of the main reasons for the Dolphins' swift turnaround. The consideration of that prestige honor has many Dolphin fans anticipating the future of the franchise. In just a few short seasons, young McDaniel has the Miami Dolphins on the brink of something very special.

When I think of coach McDaniel, I think about how he basically transformed the Dolphins into a playoff team for two consecutive seasons. I like the fact that McDaniel seems relatable as a coach. Since, he has been at the helm, the Dolphins have had flashes of seemingly good potential.

McDaniel has eclipsed the potential of creating his own culture of success. As an optimist, I believe that he can coach the team to many successful seasons. Hopefully, the coach can recreate his own coaching longevity with the Miami Dolphins in a similar way the late great coach Don Shula did.

I am a firm believer in the saying that says "It's not where you start, but how you finish." The coaching era of Mike McDaniel has commenced well, thus far. It is trending in the right direction. A bright and promising future seems realistic in the Mike McDaniel era.

Making the playoffs for two consecutive years is an accomplishment. Cosmetically, the 2023 regular season record of the Miami Dolphins was more than amazing. It was downright wonderful.

In the N.F.L., it is difficult to win only one game. Teams that are young like the current Miami Dolphins typically suffer from growing pains. Sometimes, it might take more than three to four years, for a young football team to eventually grow and blossom.

Honestly, I did not envision the young Miami Dolphins team to experience the amount of success that it has experienced in a relatively short time. Still, the Dolphins as a young and talented team must not grow complacent. The A.F.C. East is shaping up to become one of the most highly competitive divisions in all of football.

From top to bottom, each team within the division could make a case for improvement. The new era of the Miami Dolphins will hopefully consist of more divisional championships and Super Bowl appearances. This organization should be hungry for more than just being competitive with the elite teams in the N.F.L. by playing competitive games against them, or becoming close to defeating them.

Now is the time for the Miami Dolphins to continue to improve and build upon their team chemistry. The more that the young players play together, the better the chemistry will be between them when they play. Soon, those young players will transition into seasoned veterans.

Once young players become seasoned veterans it is then time for the players to understand how to play with one another. There is always expectation that comes with every N.F.L. team before every season. Since, the Dolphins have improved tremendously in the past few seasons, it is now expected that the Dolphins should become a winning franchise again.

Under coach McDaniel and general manager, Chris Grier's direction, the Dolphins have positioned themselves to finally have success for many seasons to come. These men understand what it takes for a team to become a winner.

Grier has also worked his way through the various ranks of the Dolphins' organization as an area scout to now becoming one of the most daring general managers in the N.F.L.

He was with the Dolphins when the franchise last won a playoff game. Also, Grier has been part of the scouting department for the Miami Dolphins through the franchise's worst season in team history, as well as through its many seasons of transformation with coaches and players. Teaming these two men together has resulted in the new era of the Miami Dolphins becoming more likely to result in the resurgence of a new winning culture and tradition.

What I have gathered the most about the Miami Dolphins in the past few seasons is the team's attitude of resilience. Instead of making excuses, in the new Dolphins era under coach McDaniel, excuses are not tolerated. Going into another season with the Miami Dolphins, the offensive-guru coach has the team developing his calm and winning personality.

Rebuilding a team into a successful winner is difficult. Before and also during the 2019 season, it seemed as though the Dolphins would be in many years of being in a rebuilding mode. I am certain that many Dolphin fans were bracing themselves for many seasons of losing.

Thanks to bold and aggressive moves by general manager, Chris Grier, he has given coach McDaniel the type of players who fits the mold of a Miami Dolphin under coach McDaniel's regime. Now, these men I would imagine owe their opportunity to become high- ranking minorities at positions that are mostly held by non-minorities in the National Football League to current Dolphins owner, Mr. Stephen M. Ross. In 2009, Ross became 95% owner of the Miami Dolphins.

Under the ownership of Ross, the Miami Dolphins' home stadium, now named, "Hard Rock Stadium" has received plenty of renovations and improvements. In 2016, an open-air canopy was developed in order to protect Dolphin fans from the extreme heat in South Florida at home games, especially, in the month of September when the heat in Southern Florida is the greatest. No one who is affiliated with the Miami Dolphins wants to win more than Dolphins' owner, Stephen Ross.

Viewing the Miami Dolphins from afar, Ross seems sincere when he says that he has a desire for the Dolphins to be amongst the National Football League's most successful franchises and organizations. Paraphrasing from a comment the owner made several years ago, I can recall him stating that he would like for the Miami Dolphins to win a Super Bowl before he perishes. Mr. Ross, to my knowledge is an owner who has given his franchise every opportunity to become successful.

He is willing to spend money on players who will help the Miami Dolphins continue on the franchise's winning path and tradition. In an unprecedented move, Ross has allowed notable entertainers and sports stars, such as, local and Cuban mega-star, Gloria Estefan, top-selling salsa and three-time Grammy Award winner, Marc Anthony, and sisters and tennis sensations, Venus and Serena Williams as minority owners of the Fins. It is to my knowledge that Ross has done everything within his power to make the Miami Dolphins relevant and competitive, on and off the field.

In 2021, the Miami Dolphins opened the Baptist Health Training Complex at the west side of Hard Rock Stadiums' complex. This move under the ownership of Ross is a state-of-the-art facility, and the permanent home for the team. In addition, the complex also serves as the team's headquarters.

Since owner Stephen Ross' direction, the Dolphins have frankly not been able to enjoy consistency in winning as much as the team did in previous years. I personally do not feel that Mr. Ross is responsible for the Miami Dolphins not being able to experience prolonged success. With the addition of young talent, which Mr. Ross has entrusted to the roster shaping of general manager, Chris Grier, and head coach, Mike McDaniel, there is a chance that the Miami Dolphins are trending upward.

Doing what is required to win is what every N.F.L. team should be willing to do. The Miami Dolphins are a franchise that seems like it is ready to win. The new era of Dolphins football looks promising.

In the past few years, the Dolphins have been steadily building the team through the draft and free agency. The young nucleus of talent on offense, beginning with quarterback Tua Tagovailoa, wide receivers Jaylen Waddle, Tyreek Hill, and running backs, Raheem Mostert and De'Von Achane, will continue to help the Dolphins maintain their status as an explosive offense. Miami has also stacked the offensive line with players who have the potential to anchor the line for many years to come.

With the 18th pick of the 2020 N.F. L. draft, the Dolphins picked offensive tackle, Austin Jackson out of the University of Southern California.

Next, with the 39th pick, the Dolphins drafted interior offensive lineman, Robert Hunt out of the University of Louisiana. It was plain to see that the Dolphins were building their offense through the drafting of the big guys up front. Some might not like the fact that the Dolphins were drafting so many offensive linemen, but as a football enthusiast, I believe that picking a plethora of linemen is both smart and necessary.

A team must build from the inside out. Interior offensive and defensive linemen, who play in what is commonly known to most football experts and fans as "the trenches", is vital to any N.F.L. team's success. Many who are close followers of the National Football League are cognizant of the fact that many games that are played in the N.F.L. are won and lost within "the trenches."

Most elite teams are solid within their offensive and defensive lines. Those men who play those positions do not typically bring fans to the stadium. Fans who are not as enthusiastic about the game of football might not pay attention to those big guys in the trenches that are responsible for keeping the quarterback clean and upright.

This philosophy of building the team by stockpiling on offensive linemen might not be the most popular philosophy in building a winner, but I believe that a team that has talented offensive lineman will eventually pay off in the end. Offensive lineman, are in many instances, unsung heroes. They do not always receive the credit for helping a team become victorious on Sundays, but quarterbacks and running backs will always realize their significance, as well as the importance of when their play is solid.

Offensive line play has hurt the Dolphins in previous years. When the Miami Dolphins were a perennial playoff team and competing in Super Bowls, it was the team's offensive line play that helped propel the team into one of the National Football League's most talented and elite teams. The Miami Dolphins in this new era of the franchise, essentially, looks like a franchise that is willing to do what it takes to compete with the elite franchises in the N.F.L. by how they are preparing for the next season commencing with the draft.

Culture is extremely vital to an organization's success. In previous years, after the retirements of Hall of Fame coaches, Don Shula and Jimmy Johnson, the Miami Dolphins did not have a culture of winning on a consistent basis. The Dolphins' culture of winning has taken a significant hit.

It is never a positive culture when the team is not in unison when it comes to how each member of the team views preparation and success. All members of an N.F.L. franchise must become committed to what it takes to win at all costs. That is if the cost of winning is well within the rules.

Winning on a continual basis starts and ends with the team's culture. For many seasons, the successful culture of the Dolphins past was not a top priority for some former Dolphin players. Now I am not saying that all former members of the Dolphins were guilty of not giving their full effort on the field, but some kind of way their effort did not equate to winning on a consistent basis.

We all are aware that winning is infectious. The fortunes of a particular franchise are shaped by the shared and common attitudes of the members of that organization. From the front office, coaching staff, down to the players, all of these individuals must share the same common mindset to winning football games.

In this new era of Dolphins football, I am gradually seeing the team under current head coach, Mike McDaniel, rebuilding a culture of winning and success. Players have to buy in to what the head coach and his staff are suggesting is the right approach to winning. Building a winning culture typically comes into fruition when the team has more than two consecutive winning seasons.

As of now, the Dolphins have the potential of having another consecutive winning season when the 2024 N.F.L. season commences. Miami has the players to carry out the winning culture, but it has to begin with discipline and team unity on and off the field. No one can force any of the members of the Dolphins organization to have shared characteristics of a winner.

The common goal for any N.F.L. franchise is to reach the ultimate game, the Super Bowl. Front office members, as well as the other members of the organization who are in the midst of the battles on the field must never lose sight of that one common goal. Having those same goals of reaching and then winning the Super Bowl should always become a part of the team's plan.

Successful organizations and franchises in the N.F.L. are not satisfied with only making it into the playoff tournament. They desire more than just being runner- ups in the Conference Championship game. Their eyes are collectively on the ultimate prize, and that is a Lombardy Trophy at season's end.

A team's culture of winning is a process when the majority of the team is young. When it comes to the Dolphins' franchise culture of winning, it is still in the infancy stage. These new and talented players are good individually, but those same individuals must learn how to adopt the team concept in order to sustain a winning culture.

Loving the game of football is vital to any player's success. In life, if an individual loves something then he or she will desire to do that activity on a regular basis. When it comes to the game of professional football, many claim that it is a business.

As a fan and an individual on the outside looking in, in regard to the business of football, loyalty is typically not emphasized. With each team's option of picking up the 5th year option of a player that the team drafted, it is all about results and productivity. The National Football League does stand for "Not for long" when a player under performs on the field.

There was a plethora of drafted players who were drafted by the Dolphins in previous years that for whatever reason did not pan out. It is difficult to talk and discuss a winning culture when the team's draft picks are no longer a member of the team. Drafting the right player for a particular franchise is not always reliable, or in many cases, not an exact science.

My hope for the Dolphins organization in the future is for the players that they drafted have the desire to want to remain playing for the Miami Dolphins organization. I am aware that the N.F.L. is a business. A team that offers a player more money than his current team is always appealing.

Loyalty and money are usually not synonymous with one another. In fact, they are each other's antithesis. It is quite tempting for a free-agent player to bolt to another team when the money is good.

Some players feel that they might not have the opportunity to make an enormous amount of money ever again in their playing career. In my opinion, when a player sometimes sells out for money, the "grass is not always greener on the other side." Also, I am fully aware that free agency is also a part of the modern N.F.L.

There are some free agents who have signed with another franchise for less money. Then, there are other free agents who wanted to sign with a particular team in order to play with a certain player/and or players, or become coached by a coach who has a winning culture with the team or a history of success.

The Dolphins need to have players who want to play for them. This could be accomplished and come into realization when the culture of the team has improved from the negative state that it was previously in. There is something brewing within the new era of the Dolphins that has the potential for the franchise to become more than just competitive, but a franchise that a player has a desire to play for.

Thus far, the Miami Dolphins have been a team that has again become a desired landing spot for players to join in free agency. Think about it. The team has a coach that has helped change the team's culture and mentality.

Also, there are plenty of young and talented core of players who have contributed to the team's new- found success. Once the combination of young players and veterans learn how to play and mesh together, there is no limit to the potential of the tremendous amount of success that the Dolphins franchise could experience. If the Dolphins can discover more players who will choose team success over money, then the path to success in this new era of the Miami Dolphins will continue to grow.

This new era of Dolphins football will hopefully help the franchise become restored to its former glory. Success is acquired when there is the determination and the motivation to succeed. The Miami Dolphins organization cannot erase its past seasons of success, but the team and organization cannot also rely upon past accomplishments.

A future of new success will help the franchise write its own narrative. Although, the 1972 Miami Dolphins will always be a part of Dolphins' history, as well as embedded in the history of the N.F.L., the new era of Dolphins football could create new memories. Dolphin fans have waited many years for the team to once again become "leaders of the pack."

Winning a playoff game in 2024 is the first step for the Miami Dolphins to begin another tradition of winning. The Dolphins have had minimal success as a team in recent years. Though, success has not been consistent, I am still anticipating how well the team will play on both sides of the ball in the upcoming season.

When it comes to success in the N.F.L., all teams are judged by their ability to win Super Bowls. Potential does not always equate to success and victories. The Dolphins have the potential to win the A.F.C. East for the first time since the 2008 N.F.L. season, but the team must not allow these past two seasons of success to cause them to regress into a state of complacency, as well as becoming unmotivated.

I believe that coach Mike McDaniel will not allow being complacent and unmotivated to become responsible for the team's lack of success. Many of the players who were drafted by the Dolphins coming out of college, essentially come from "blue-blood" college programs. College programs that are considered "blue-blooded" are programs, which have a long and prosperous tradition of winning.

Most players who come from those institutions in which winning is the norm are highly competitive. Also, these players are used to competing on a high level. Once the players from "blue-blood" schools reach the National Football League, the bright lights of the N.F.L. are not a bothersome distraction.

The Miami Dolphins have in recent N.F.L. drafts, drafted young college prospects from college programs that are familiar with winning. It makes sense to draft young talent from schools, which are always in the national spotlight. College programs that win on a consistent basis also have a low tolerance for losing.

In the N.F.L., typically, there is not much separation in talent. This is why football has been known in the past for being 90% mental and 10% physical. Intelligent players play the game on a high level, and are typically the team's best players.

They can pinpoint things on the field that some coaches might not become aware of until it is time to study film. Hopefully, the Dolphins drafting of intelligent players from "blue-blood" programs will ultimately pay off. As fans, we will all know when the Dolphins new era of football is successful when the franchise can gain more victories on a regular basis, and the team is able to advance past the Wild Card and Divisional playoff game, into the game of all games, which ends in a World Championship.

CHAPTER 9
The Dolphins should have motivation to win

Divisional runner-ups, losing consistently in the Wild Card round of the N.F.L. playoffs, as well as the team's inability to have prolonged success are just some of the main factors that should motivate the Miami Dolphins to win. The members of the Dolphins' front office have set the team up to finally win, but it is ultimately up to the new nucleus of young Dolphin talent to help propel the franchise away from its mediocre status. During the Dolphins twenty plus years of mediocrity, I have been patiently waiting for the team to become a perennial contender.

Once a team becomes motivated to win, in many instances, that team can essentially become unstoppable. The professional football team who hails from South Florida should not have any difficulty in trying to become motivated. All the Dolphins have to do is look at the other divisional rivals within the division.

The other three divisional opponents have had some playoff success, whereas the Miami Dolphins have not. In recent years, the Dolphins have lost games in the final weeks of the season. In past seasons, if the Dolphins could have won at least one or two of those remaining games, it could have resulted in the team making the playoffs.

I am also aware that teams who make the playoffs have another incentive to advance well into the playoff tournament. That incentive is no other than money. Teams who advance to the Super Bowl are given extra pay by the National Football League just by winning extra games.

Players who are fortunate enough to play in the N.F.L. should not only be motivated by a huge paycheck. The minimum salary of an N.F.L. veteran is still lucrative. These men who play a "child's game" are handsomely paid regardless of how their respective team finishes.

Maybe this has been the attitude and mindset of some Dolphin players in the past. Instead of being motivated to win games, some have elected to only play for individual incentives. When a player only plays for incentives that will only benefit him, ultimately the team will suffer.

The game of football is the ultimate team sport. Each member of a team must be motivated to win in order for the team to experience any type of team success. Players, who play selfishly, do not fit into the team concept that is very crucial in order for the team to become victorious on Sundays.

Previously, I discussed how the Dolphins have recently picked players from "college football factories." Many of these young players who come from schools that win a majority of its games will hate to lose. Losing can give players who are used to winning the motivation to continue to win.

New Miami Dolphins players who come from winning college football programs will not lack the motivation and the incentive to win now. In the defense of current young players who were drafted by the team, they are far removed from the previous Dolphin teams of the past that lacked the will to win. Simply enjoying all the perks of winning should be enough motivation for the new breed of Dolphins players.

Defense sets the tone for many teams in the National Football League. If the team's defense is solid, then the team could be in a position to win many of its games. I have yet to see a Super Bowl team win without a viable defense.

Part of the Miami Dolphins' issues for years have been lack of motivation on the team's defensive unit. I have heard players and commentators in the past describe the Dolphins' defensive side of the ball as "soft." When a professional football team is labeled "soft" that essentially means that the defense cannot stop the running game of the opposing team.

Also, a "soft" label means that the defense does not have defenders who are willing to tackle the opposing team's power running back. Not only does the "bruiser" of a running back will have his way on a team's "soft" defense, but the rest of the offense, the quarterbacks, wide receivers, and offensive linemen could impose their will to score on a defense that is considered "soft."

When opposing offensive teams state to the media, as well as amongst themselves that an opposing defense is "soft" that should be taken as an insult and motivation to not allow the opposing offense to become more physical than the team's opposing defensive unit, whom they are playing.

On most of the Miami Dolphins' Super Bowl contending teams, those teams had physical defenses. The only Dolphin team that was the exception of a physical defense was the last team to reach the Super Bowl for the Miami Dolphins, which was the 1984 team. Led by Marino and the Marks Brothers, the 1984 team was primarily carried by the offensive side of the ball.

It was before and after that Super Bowl defeat in which the Dolphins experienced that I initially heard of the term "soft." Personally, I believe that a physical defense is an attitude and mentality. A team must have the right caliber of players in order to be considered a defense that is physical.

The Dolphins' defensive unit should be motivated to erase that "soft" label, which has plagued the team for many years.

Passion and the willingness to make a tackle are key factors of a defense not having the "soft" label. With the defensive acquisitions of unheralded defensive lineman Christian Wilkins, defensive ends Bradley Chubb and Jaelan Phillips, linebackers Jerome Baker, Duke Riley, and lastly perennial all-pro cornerback Jaylen Ramsey, the Dolphins' defense has made significant strides in shedding that negative "soft" label.

If the Miami Dolphins could continue to improve defensively with controlled passion and aggression, then I believe that the Dolphins can finally shake the "soft label" on the defensive side of the ball. 2024 should be the year that could be the determining factor in regard to whether or not that motivation to become a physical defense finally did come into fruition. In my opinion, defense really is responsible for Super Bowl wins, although an offense, which can score touchdowns and sustain scoring drives on offense, is also imperative. A Dolphins' defense that can stop the run, gang tackle, keep the opposing offense's scoring opportunities to a minimum, while also playing with passion on a consistent basis, is definitely a defense that is motivated to carry the team to undeniable success.

No one can play professional football effectively without having some semblance of motivation. Someway and somehow, the Miami Dolphins must continue to improve and play inspired football. The Dolphins have to channel all of those years of finishing second behind those two A.F.C. East dynasties, into winning football games.

As a fan, although I do not perform on the field, I am motivated as a fan for the Miami Dolphins to have more than one season of winning more than nine games within a season. If I was a player on the Dolphins, I would grow tired of hearing about all of the other teams in the National Football League who are supposed to compete for Lombardy Trophies each year. The mention of another team in the A.F.C. East that many experts believe are Super Bowl contenders, such as, the Buffalo Bills, for example, would provide the needed fuel and motivation to beat them.

Football games are won and lost in the off-season these days. A team has to bring in the right caliber of player, whether a particular player is picked in the N.F.L. draft, or he is signed as a free agent, that player who will practice in the team's facility must have the same motivation to win just as much as the new player's teammates, who are already on the team. Some players say that they avoid reading newspapers, as well as listening to the news media.

This is a difficult thing to do when reporters are all around the team searching for answers to what happened on a certain play. It is by word of mouth, or in this current social media climate, the stroke of a keyboard on a computer, that a player can immediately learn about what others are saying about them, or the team, first-hand. I would be motivated as a player if I read on a social media outlet, or saw on a sports show that my team was not good enough to win or beat a particular opponent.

Also, it would motivate me to play hard when social media outlets, and sports programs were not mentioning the team that I play for. When it comes to motivation, it should not take much to have it. Along with motivation for a team to win, is the desire for that team to prove others wrong.

In my opinion, the Miami Dolphins as a team, definitely have what it takes to silence those critics who do not envision the team building upon what they did the previous season. The Dolphins' mantra going into the upcoming season should be "Why not us? There is always some type of motivation that each team could use to bolster them into playing beyond their potential. For many seasons, frankly, the Dolphins have taken a "backseat" to other teams in the N.F.L. regarding relevancy.

If experts and critics are not mentioning how well that a team is playing, then that team does not have any kind of clout. Teams, which are worth mentioning by those around the National Football league are not average, or "middle of the pack teams." In fact, there are two type of teams that most critics deem worth mentioning, and that is a playoff caliber, Super Bowl contending team, or a team that is believed to be dreadful. All of the Miami Dolphins players should have motivation to become mentioned as a Super Bowl contender, instead of a team that is dismal.

Second-best, typically does not qualify for being "number one" in anything in life. In most instances, the average person does not remember who finished second in anything. Previously, in chapter seven, I mentioned how the Dolphins seemed that they were always just a step below the front-runner in their division.

Honestly, the New England Patriots are the envy of just about every team in the National Football League. The winning tradition and culture of the New England Patriots, within the past two decades, could be compared to no one. Maybe the Cleveland Browns in the 1950s could come close to the Patriots dynasty.

Cleveland won their division in the old National Football League for six straight seasons, while winning three World Championships in that span. Years after the Browns dynasty, no one could have imagined that another franchise's N.F.L. dominance would surpass them enormously. New England's dominance in the A.F.C. Eastern division, as well as throughout the National Football League is quite the accomplishment.

The Patriots had won the A.F.C. East for a record 11 straight seasons, while also compiling three Super Bowl wins during that span. They have won without having the boisterous or flashy athletes. Bill Belichick's teams just line up and play fundamentally sound football.

As a fan of the Miami Dolphins primarily the majority of my life, I never thought that a team within the A.F.C. East would enjoy that type of unprecedented, and unparalleled success. It motivates me as a Dolphins fan to see the day when the Miami Dolphins have divisional dominance within the A.F.C. East. One way that the Dolphins can ensure that the Bills dominant reign on the A.F.C. East is over is by beating them with regularity.

Every team within the A.F.C. East division should have motivation to knock off the current divisional dynasty for good, especially, the Miami Dolphins. Think about it. A team that has dominated the division for consecutive seasons, and you are basically the team that typically finishes behind them in the A.F.C. East divisional standings should become enough motivation to beat them, while also striving to build their own lasting dynasty.

For many seasons, the Miami Dolphins have had a "front-row seat" to the New England Patriots reign of supremacy within the division and in the playoffs. The Patriots have also appeared in the most Super Bowls ever with nine appearances. In many of the seasons that the Patriots have won the division, those Patriots teams have had the luxury of earning home field advantage throughout the playoff tournament. Due to their winning advantage in their home stadium, most teams did not come out with a victory when they played at the Gillette Stadium in Foxborough, Massachusetts in previous seasons.

The Miami Dolphins should have motivation to have another home field advantage like the one they had in the former Orange Bowl Stadium in much of the early years of the Don Shula era. Visiting teams dreaded coming down to the heat and humidity of Southern Florida. In recent years, due to the Dolphins' mediocre play, most fans and visiting teams have treated playing in Hard Rock Stadium in Miami, Florida as a vacation and destination spot, instead of a place where the opposing team is bound to lose.

Elite franchises do what is required to win in their own home stadium. If you look at the elite teams around the

National Football League, they have some sort of home-field mystique when opposing teams play them at home. As I previously stated, the Dolphins do not have an on-going competitive advantage anymore.

It seems as though fans and opponents have anticipated the warm beaches and weather in Miami, Florida. These days, the heat and humidity of South Florida seems like a welcomed attraction, especially, if those opposing teams who the Dolphins play are coming from a region of frigid and inclement weather. Fan support could become vital to a team's success.

Any coach in sports would tell his team that they have to "protect the home field." Protecting the home field means that the home team goes out on their home field with intentions of winning the game in their home stadium. The team that protects the home field the best are typically the elite teams.

Opposing fans that go into an opposing stadium, in which few have won, will become intimidated by many of the other opposing team's lack of success. In the back of the minds of the visiting team, although they support their team, they still know that the team that is "good at protecting the home field" will most likely win the game, although the opposing team has infiltrated the stadium with their fans. Sadly, when it comes to my beloved Miami Dolphins, Dolphin fans have not always filled the stadium.

Some have elected not to support the team in the Miami heat. Many fans do not feel the need to support the Miami Dolphins in their home stadium because for starters, they could be doing other fun activities on Sundays in the city of Miami, such as, taking a boat ride in the Atlantic Ocean, or relaxing on the beach. Lastly, there are some Dolphins fans that do not want to experience the uncertainty of winning.

Because in recent years, the Dolphins have not enjoyed an overwhelming competitive advantage at home, the fan support for the team has waned. When there is not any cause for excitement by the team's play, many will not make it their priority to attend Dolphins' home games. They might say to themselves that there are other things that I could be doing with my time rather than seeing the Dolphins not winning on a regular basis at home.

This particular attitude and mindset would help motivate me greatly if I were a Miami Dolphins player or coach. A team that plays to an unlimited amount of fans are generally those teams, which are thriving. Fans will support a winning team no matter how extreme the elements are.

In the late 1990s, that was the last time that I could recall the Miami Dolphins having a stadium filled with screaming Dolphins fans. Since then, fan attendance to Miami Dolphins home games has gradually dwindled over time. Winning consistently at home will once again help the Dolphins become considered as one of the National Football League's most successful teams. Bringing fans into the stadium is enough motivation for the team to play its best.

Oh-no not again! The Miami Dolphins might be saying internally as a franchise. I believe the reason why they could be saying that phrase is due to the potential resurgence of the Buffalo Bills. In 2023, the Bills won the A.F.C. East crown. They made the playoffs in each season since 2019.

Although, they lost the 2021 A.F.C. Championship game to the Super Bowl runner-up, the Kansas City Chiefs, 38 to 24, the Bills seem as though they will become a force again in both the A.F.C. East, as well as in the A.F.C. Conference. The Dolphins lost an important game to the Buffalo Bills in the 2023 regular season finale. This particular game proves how the mentality of the Miami Dolphins must change in order to win those all-important games.

The Bills stood in the way between the Dolphins' chances of winning the division and having a home playoff game.

In recent years, the Buffalo Bills have enjoyed a plethora of success against the Dolphins. There should be an enormous amount of self-evaluation for the Dolphins organization.

Also, to make matters worse, the Bills swept the Dolphins for the second time in three seasons. Dolphin fans might be thinking to themselves, the Buffalo Bills are a team that is now prominent on the Miami Dolphins radar.

Motivating a Dolphins' team to victory should not become difficult for Dolphin head coach, Mike McDaniel when it comes to playing the Buffalo Bills again. Miami has played a plethora of lackluster games against the team from Western, New York, the Buffalo Bills in recent seasons.

If that is not enough motivation to win, then I do not know what else could serve as motivation for the Miami Dolphins. 2024 will be a test for the Dolphins as to whether or not the team was able to overcome the losing woes in which the Buffalo Bills have caused. Buffalo seems as though they are poised to take the next step in the A.F.C. Conference by setting themselves up to challenge the mighty Kansas City Chiefs, who are led by superstar quarterback, Patrick Mahomes. For the talented Buffalo Bills, there is not much improvement as a team that they have to make.

What the Miami Dolphins have working in their favor is the fact that they also are a young and talented team. Under current coach, Mike McDaniel, they have seemed to make significant improvement from the coach's first year. There is a positive energy that I sense from the Dolphins that I have not sensed in a long time. The young and talented Miami Dolphins should be motivated to beat the Buffalo Bills because that team is standing in the way of the Dolphins' turn to become the team to conquer the A.F.C. Eastern division.

1973 was the last season that the Miami Dolphins experienced a Super Bowl victory. I was born in that year, and it amazes me that I am as old as the last Lombardy Trophy the

Dolphins have ever had. Gone are some of the players and coaches who made that Super Bowl victory possible.

Before the Kansas City Chiefs won Super Bowl LIV over the San Francisco 49ers, 31 to 20, it had been 50 seasons since the Chiefs last Super Bowl victory in Super Bowl IV. The Chiefs, members of the former American Football League, won that game in 1970, 23 to 7, over the National Football League's, Minnesota Vikings in my hometown of New Orleans, at the old Tulane Stadium, which is the home of Tulane's college football squad, the Green Wave. I have mentioned the Kansas City Chiefs because by them winning another Super Bowl, 50 seasons later, it could offer hope for Dolphins fans.

Of course, the Dolphins have been in the big game twice since 1973 (1982,1984), but unfortunately, for the Dolphins, they came up short. The Chiefs, on the other hand, were not as fortunate as the Miami Dolphins to appear in the ultimate game as many times as the Dolphins have appeared, until recently. Still, the Dolphins are long overdue for a Super Bowl appearance and victory.

Also, the Chiefs began their dominance in the A.F.C. West approximately seven seasons ago. After experiencing back-to- back losing seasons in 2011 and 2012, the Chiefs hired a new head coach, which was veteran head- man, coach Andy Reid. In Reid's first full season with the team, they finished in second place. It would become a recurring theme for Andy Reid coached teams because the Chiefs finished three consecutive seasons in 2nd place before they finally captured the A.F.C. Western division in 2016.

You, the reader, might be thinking to yourself " Why is he mentioning the Kansas City Chiefs in a book about the Miami Dolphins and the team's divisional rivals?" I am mentioning the Chiefs organization because (a) I see parallels between the Chiefs and Dolphins franchises (b) both teams endured multiple years of second-place finishes (c) they are an example of what patience and hope could result in when the owner and fan base gives the coach time to build a winner.

The Miami Dolphins could also follow that same winning pattern as the Kansas City Chiefs have. That team's success was gradual, and it did not occur immediately. The Chiefs had to learn how to win after losing repetitively in the A.F.C. Wild Card and Divisional playoffs in successive seasons.

After losing the A.F.C. Championship to the eventual Super Bowl champions, the New England Patriots, they (the Kansas City Chiefs) would finally "get over the hump" in the very next year. The Chiefs had to learn how to become an N.F.L. powerhouse team. Once they were able to capture first place within their division, they have not relinquished their divisional crown for several years. The Dolphins could look at the Chiefs improvement over the years and become motivated instantly by the team's recent success.

Starting out fast in the first few weeks of the season for the Dolphins has been the team's strength recently. In 2022, the Dolphins began the season with three straight wins. This trend also occurred in the 2023 season. Although, the team started well, the Dolphins still finished the season with a losing streak and another early playoff exit.

Dolphin fans have to think that if the team had finished December and January strong, they would have found themselves in the playoffs without having to put themselves in a plethora of pressure to win in the last regular season game of the season. In my opinion, if the Dolphins can tweak their mentality in regard to their mind-set in the big games, the team could become a force in the league.

Historically, the Dolphins have not started the season well. There were some seasons under legendary coach, Don Shula that the Dolphins got off to a poor start. This current Dolphins' team has started out well, but by seasons' end, the team finished poorly.

Each passing season, I am always reminded about how the Dolphins must strive to win their last few games in December. If Miami wants to be considered among the elite teams, then a great finish must occur. When a team is consistent throughout the season, they do not have to worry about scoreboard watching in the season's last week.

Teams that are elite, typically, have the division wrapped up prior to the last game of the regular season. The Dolphins' motivation should be to start fast to set the tone. Starting fast, and maintaining it throughout the season alleviates worry.

I am aware of the fact that winning one game in the National Football League is no small feat. Because the talent league-wide is almost identical within every various position, a player's motivation to excel is what will propel that player to play his best. Of course, there is not an" I" in team.

Games are won and lost as a team, not as individuals. The Dolphins have drafted enough individual talent to compete within the division. But in the N.F.L., talent alone will not always catapult a team into playoff contention.

Now I am not saying that the Dolphins should disregard all the talented players that they have accumulated. What I am saying is that when all of a team's individual talent can somehow manage to play together as a team, that team will enjoy success. Each member of the Miami Dolphins must know collectively what is at stake when the team begins and ends the season on a roll.

Talent, team unity, and motivation working together simultaneously could make a team play well, and become special. Once those team attributes are established, then the team is on its way to having a winning culture. Before a winning tradition can formulate, all of the team's members must become motivated as a team to do whatever it takes to win consistently. Most elite teams that are motivated to win do not care about individual statistics and accolades.

Critics and skeptics always have an opinion. There is not anything that a professional sports team can do to silence them, except prove them wrong and win. Many critics of the Miami Dolphins have pointed out the team's mediocre play in the last few decades.

I must admit that I agree with some of them. We all know that critics could sometimes give a harsh opinion. In many cases, the truth hurts.

The Miami Dolphins have not always played to their potential. I believe that part of the blame could be placed on the previous coaching staffs, but in the National Football League, a player cannot always rely upon a coach to motivate him. He has to be self-motivated to play his best.

In the past, the Dolphins have had talented players to grace their facility. As a fan I have seen some of them move on to other franchises and become successful. There were times that I would wonder why that player did not play that well when he was with the Miami Dolphins? In my opinion, the new era of the Miami Dolphins must not hold on to successes of season's past.

Sure, in 2023 the Dolphins surprised many skeptics and critics around the N.F.L. when they commenced to be mentioned amongst the elite teams of the N.F.L. for much of the season. But 2023 is gone, and there is another season that is upon us. According to many circles in the N.F.L., the Dolphins are now viewed as a franchise on the rise.

When I hear the term "on the rise" I honestly think about potential. That word potential to me is not always a positive word, especially, when it comes to the Dolphins. Some who claim that the Dolphins have potential to become an A.F.C. powerhouse team are not wrong.

In fact, every team in the off-season, and before the start of the season has potential to become a good team. It is because of that known fact that players and coaches should not become satisfied with their progress. They should be motivated to want more than just a few critics discussing the team's potential to become an elite caliber team.

Success in the N.F.L. is not given it is earned. Those men who make up the Miami Dolphins roster must be motivated to win if they want to erase the mediocre label that critics and skeptics have bestowed on them. The Dolphins must also become motivated not to take a step back from last year's playoff run.

If the Dolphins do regress from their strong 2023 season, then the critics will say that the strong campaign was a fluke. The Miami Dolphins have many things to motivate them to experience another season of success. First, they have to try to keep the entire A.F.C. East in check.

Next, they have to find a way to overcome the resurging Buffalo Bills. Then, they have to try to establish themselves as a team that is more than just potential. In other words, the Miami Dolphins must be motivated to win now.

A division title should become the main reason why the Dolphins should be motivated to win. They have not won the division in sixteen years. With the threat of the Buffalo Bills becoming an elite team in the entire American Football Conference, and a threat in the N.F.L. again, the Dolphins should have the motivation to overcome those threats.

Improvement and resurgence are what should motivate the Miami Dolphins in the up-coming season. They have to first become a team, instead of a team made up of individuals who just happens to play for the team. All of the players on the roster should be motivated to continue to improve and get better.

Although, the Dolphins have not been a dismal team in recent years, they also have not showed up in "big games". The Dolphins should be motivated not to regress to a "middle of the pack" team. At some point, the team has to improve from being average.

Average in the N.F.L. is dull and boring. No team should be satisfied with being an average team. This is why the Dolphins should become motivated to shake that "average label."

The bottom line for the Miami Dolphins is that in recent years, many teams around the N.F.L. have passed them by. There was a time that the Dolphins were a team and franchise that was being hunted by other franchises, in regard to being a model of consistency because in the past the Dolphins were a good team year in and year out. Now, the Miami Dolphins are one of those organizations and teams that are looking at other organizations to model themselves after.

Though, the Dolphins have a model of success within their own division in the New England Patriots, and recently, the Buffalo Bills, they (the Dolphins) cannot fully emulate them. The Dolphins franchise and organization has to become motivated to forge their own unique pattern of success and longevity. For many seasons, the Dolphins have not been able to develop their own winning formula.

As the years have gone by, the Miami Dolphins have not been a team and organization in which most organizations would desire to pattern themselves after. Honestly, when it comes to all of the minority hires in the top positions within the Dolphins franchise, it is something that many N.F.L. teams should strive to follow. That is commendable, but what ultimately counts is the product on the field.

The Miami Dolphins organization has experienced lean times in the 21st century. With the team's successful rebuild, the Dolphins should be motivated to change that pattern of unsuccessfulness and mediocrity. Looking at the big picture, the teams in the A.F.C. and around the National Football

League have not looked at the Dolphins as a team that invokes fear.

Teams could have been viewing the Dolphins as "pushovers" rather than a team that requires the utmost respect. When the Miami Dolphins learn how to win with consistency, then teams will learn how to have more respect for the Dolphins when they play them. Earning the respect in regard to longevity in winning is enough motivation for the Miami Dolphins to play inspired football. Winning and motivation go hand and hand, and a team that is motivated to win, as a team, will silence the critics and the doubters when all of the dust settles.

CHAPTER 10
Are the Days of Glory Ahead?

Longing for the days of yesteryear will not do the current Miami Dolphins franchise any good. When it comes to longing for something, it could generally equate to a desire. Desiring something is one thing, but turning that desire into realization is another.

From the 1970s until the very beginning of the 21st century, the Miami Dolphins were that model franchise. It was during that span that the Dolphins did not go more than four years without being one of the teams that was in playoff contention. I do not have to reiterate the limited amount of success of the Miami Dolphins in the last several years because that is a known fact and reality.

These current Dolphin teams could help the team become glorified again. In the past, the best Dolphins teams were intimidating on the defensive side of the ball. Currently, the Dolphins have a defense that is positioning itself to become a force amongst N.F.L. teams throughout the league.

Gradually, the Dolphins defense has become solid. Sure, I believe that the offensive side of the ball is important. In fact, all three phases of the game are vital to a team's longevity in success.

An elite team must have a solid offense, defense, and special teams. If all three phases are working for a team, then winning consistently will soon ensue. Defense is usually the way that a team could eventually dominate.

Keeping the opposing team from scoring, and limiting the amount of yards that the opposing team has in rushing and passing are important factors that could contribute to a reliable defense. In 2023, the Dolphins defense produced a plethora of sacks.

The Miami Dolphins are now progressing toward being a complete team based on the team's play in the 2023 N.F.L. season. Having a sound defense is one thing, but having a potent offense will help the team to become a more complete and balanced team.

Dolphin teams that were great in the past were both disciplined and intelligent. They especially had those qualities on defense. Head coach, Mike McDaniel's primary specialty as a coach is on the offensive side of the ball.

His 2022 and 2023 offensive teams were explosive at times. The Dolphins offense in some games was a joy to watch. It was a joy to see that explosive offense on display in the record-breaking 70- point game against the Denver Broncos.

Defense will keep a team in the game, and it was one of the main reasons why the Miami Dolphins was able to reach 5 Super Bowls. This side of the ball has a chance to launch the Dolphins into the long awaited glory that Dolphin fans have been patiently waiting for. If coach McDaniel could continue to help the Dolphins offense improve, then the Dolphins' future glory will soon manifest.

Bright, is what the future glory of the Miami Dolphins looks like. The team looks as though it will continue to gradually improve. Acquiring glory requires great patience and sacrifice.

The Dolphins franchise has experienced an adequate amount of glory and honor in the organization's rich history.

Each year, when the last team to lose during the N.F.L. regular season is established, the remaining members of the 1972 Miami Dolphins celebrate this glory and honor by celebrating their accomplishment by having a party or a get together. Celebrating that past glory and honor when the last team loses has been a tradition for the 1972 undefeated Miami Dolphins for many years.

Now of course, I do not know if these current Miami Dolphins players will become fortunate enough to repeat that honor. They might not finish the season by becoming undefeated. That accomplishment, regardless of whether or not another team equals that magnificent feat, will never be broken.

No one could ever erase that special season in Dolphins' history. Although, the season resulted in an unblemished, perfect, record, imperfect people helped accomplish that unprecedented record. The present Dolphins under coach McDaniel could bring the franchise another round of glory.

There are enough young and talented players who could position the Dolphins into a franchise that has the potential to experience prolonged success. But first, the young talented Dolphins must never view their youth as a hindrance. Some say that veteran teams are the most successful teams in sports.

This gives less hope to a young team because many feel that they do not know how to win. I believe that when a team is young and playing well that is an indication that the team is mature and disciplined. The Dolphins' young nucleus of talent on offense could also help bring the franchise back to an elite status.

With the drafting of talented players coming from the college ranks, the Dolphins are building their franchise to compete with the elite teams in the N.F.L. If the Miami Dolphins want to return back to past glory, they not only must win immediately, but they also must beat the teams they should beat, while also defeating the elite teams, which the team is not supposed to defeat. In addition, players and coaches have to work together for the common goal of winning games, in spite of the adversity and inner turmoil that all teams experience within a given season.

Team distractions could derail a season of promise when coaches are oblivious of many of the issues that the players encounter. When it comes to personal distractions, it is inevitable. No matter how hard a team tries to avoid them, they will typically occur at some inopportune time.

Somehow, the young talent of the Miami Dolphins must not allow distractions to affect the future glory of the team. If distractions that are detrimental to the team could have a somewhat minimal effect, then the team's success will not become influenced by it. Success and glory will only occur when the team as a whole can overcome all of the potentially threatening distractions that could have a prolonged negative effect.

2024 could serve as a catalyst for the resurgence of the Miami Dolphins. They have to continue to improve. Because of the Dolphins strong season, there are many teams who will be ready to play them.

For me as a fan, I am starting to believe that the Dolphins can finally break away from their mediocre play. They must somehow not settle, by accepting second-place finishes. If the Miami Dolphins want to be considered amongst the N.F.L. elite teams, they have to be able to beat the top teams.

After the 2023 season, I was convinced that the Dolphins are a team that could challenge for the A.F.C. East divisional title. But first, they must figure out a way to at least split the divisional games with their divisional rival, the Buffalo Bills. The task to beat the Buffalo Bills, the 2023 A.F.C. Eastern divisional champions will be difficult.

I do not expect that the New England Patriots will be a factor because they are a team in transition. You can also state that the New York Jets are also in a transitional state. And of course, the Buffalo Bills are expected to be the team to beat within the division. The Dolphins now have the coach and the players to overcome the other A.F.C. East divisional foes.

A return to glory for the Miami Dolphins commences when they are able to defeat those other teams who they play twice a year regularly, commencing with the Buffalo Bills. In order to accomplish that goal of returning to glory in the division, as well as in the entire National Football League, the Dolphins must have a prolonged hunger and desire to accomplish it. When a team is successful in the N.F.L., they are considered relevant.

No one will consider the Miami Dolphins relevant again, until they learn how to win consistently. Also, they must become a participant in the N.F.L. playoff tournament more than once every few years. There is a psychological mindset that the Dolphins must have if they want to overcome their "football demons."

It is a mindset of the Dolphins against everybody, which could help the team gain a psychological edge when they play. Having that mindset ultimately results in the team playing with "a chip on their shoulders." That mindset typically works with players who felt overlooked or slighted on their journey to play in the N.F.L.

Individuals who play with a "chip on their shoulders" do not have any problem with becoming motivated. In many instances, players who are motivated will be able to play their best each week. Teams that collectively are made up with individuals with a "chip on the shoulder" mindset will have a sense of urgency to succeed and prove the critics wrong.

The Dolphins should have that mindset after all of those years of not being good enough to challenge for a division title, as well as lack of regular appearances in the playoffs and Super Bowl. A team that plays to win will never have a problem with gaining glory. If the 2023 campaign was a synopsis of what is to come for the Miami Dolphins to experience future glory, then in the next few years, the franchise will receive its just due.

Glory and honor only comes to teams who are either regular participants of the Super Bowl, or Super Bowl champions. The Dolphins have not earned a Super Bowl berth in approximately forty years. The franchise has not had the glory and honor of being a Super Bowl champion, and that as a fan is frustrating.

I have realized as a fan that it is never easy to win a World Championship in any sport. Teams that win championships have to somehow dig deep and play their best when it counts. Unfortunately, the Dolphins have not been able to play their best in important games.

Now, the Dolphins have made the playoffs in the past few years. In fact, it has been approximately thirty-two years since they made the A.F.C. Championship. When the Miami Dolphins enter the N.F.L. post-season, it is typically one and done.

Making it into the playoff tournament should not only be a team's goal. A Super Bowl appearance must be the team's number one aspiration. It does not matter if a team makes it to the Wild Card game and loses because it would be as if the team never made the playoffs at all.

Winning teams are hungry for more than just making it to the Wild Card game. In fact, they are disappointed if they do not advance to the Super Bowl. I am not in any way stating that those Dolphins teams in the past that lost in the Wild Card game did not want to reach the Super Bowl.

It just seems as though many of the Dolphin teams that made the playoffs after losing in the Wild Card round, did not have the motivation and drive to want more than just have bragging rights that they were one of the teams who made the playoffs that particular season. I equate the Dolphins' past participation in the Wild Card playoff game to a couple that gets married. Sure, it is special when a couple has a wedding.

Just making it to the Alter is one thing, but advancing further into a marriage is another. There are some individuals who become married just to say to others that the goal of becoming married was accomplished. They have no clue what is required to remain married.

Marriage is not always pretty. The individuals who are in the marriage must sacrifice and work together each day on the commitment they made to one another. Both participants in the marriage must not stop doing the things that they did before their covenant.

I am comparing some couples that become married to a team that plays like they are just happy to play in a Wild Card game because both scenarios could become an example of complacency. Married couples that are only happy with only making it to the Alter are complacent when they do not do what it takes to have a successful marriage. After they said " I Do" it is as though some couples immediately stop trying.

The Miami Dolphins are due to have a resurgence of glory. But in order for the franchise to experience glory and honor, the team has to be willing to go above and beyond just making it into the post-season. Winning, glory, and eventually honor will only come into fruition when a team is not satisfied with nothing else other than winning a Super Bowl.

Just like the franchise itself, Dolphins fans are also anticipating the day that the organization can win another Super Bowl. Playoff appearances will not do anything to restore a franchise's glory. That franchise has to win the big game in order to become amongst the Super Bowl winning teams.

Suffering Dolphin fans want more than just a playoff berth. They would like nothing more than the Miami Dolphins becoming the last team standing after a Super Bowl victory. Super Bowl winning teams have a certain mindset and mystique about them.

It seems as though teams that win the Super Bowl are able to intensify their play as they advance throughout the playoffs. Players and coaches on Super Bowl caliber teams are laser focused on the goal at hand, which ultimately is a Super Bowl victory. With the young talent that the Dolphins have gradually developed, as well as the talented coaching staff that the Dolphins have assembled, the team is destined for glory.

I believe that the Miami Dolphins have not been far from becoming a team that could be a playoff contender for several years. For the Dolphins to go beyond just a playoff caliber team to a Super Bowl contender, the team must learn how to play their best in the months of September, December, and January. As I previous stated, the Dolphins have historically gotten off to terrible starts in the beginning of the season in September.

In order for the Miami Dolphins franchise to experience future glory, the team itself must win primarily in those months that I just mentioned. Of course, the goal should be to win throughout the whole entire season, not only in those specific months. Most Super Bowl winning teams start fast by winning the majority of their games in September, then in the months of December and early January, those teams head towards the playoffs playing their best, while gaining the momentum to advance deep into the post-season.

Advancing in the playoffs has not been the norm for the Dolphins for a plethora of seasons, but if the franchise does advance well into the post-season tournament, it will give fans hope that resurgence has taken place. The time to rekindle past glory is definitely now. It does not mean that the

Dolphins can relive the glory of the past because that era of past glory is over.

When it comes to each team in the N.F.L. success is unpredictable. A team could dramatically improve and exceed expectations, or the team could regress and disappoint their fan base. From season to season, no one could exactly predict how well their team will play, or if they will even make it to the last game of the season.

Sometimes, it might take a certain play or game that could change the direction and fortunes of a franchise. Any team could come out of nowhere to challenge for a World Championship in the N.F.L. This is why parity in the National Football League is so amazing.

The Dolphins' resurgence and glory can occur sooner rather than later. Dolphin fans are looking forward to the day when the franchise is lifting up a Super Bowl trophy. They just have to believe that the Miami Dolphins resurgence in glory is not far or out of reach.

Home-field advantages are what teams who are successful have. Previously, I briefly touched on that topic. I am revisiting the subject of home-field advantage because it is vital to all of the teams in the National Football League who want to have a competitive advantage in the post-season.

When teams win at home, their fans will grow to expect a win. There is a certain level of assurance and confidence that fans have when their team is basically unbeatable at home. The Miami Dolphins must somehow strive to regain the mystique that they once had when teams were intimidated by the heat and humidity of Miami, Florida.

In 2023, the Dolphins home record was 6 wins and 2 losses. That is not a bad home record. But if the Miami Dolphins want to be considered a team of glory, even that winning record at home has to improve.

Both of the Dolphins' home losses were close. This is what could be considered a positive take on those defeats. Also, the Dolphins lost both games by 7 points or less.

Dolphin fans should come away optimistic by how well the Dolphins fared at home in 2023. Once the team learns how to beat those elite playoff teams on the road, then the Dolphins could not only become restored to glory, but they could also be considered a dangerous team. Teams who win home games on a regular basis provide their fans hope that if the team is able to play a home game in front of the home crowd in the playoffs, their team will likely become victorious.

Sadly, when the Dolphins had previous home playoff games in the past, the outcome of the game did not end in the way that the team and their fans would have hoped. Those home defeats were blowout losses to the same opponent, the Baltimore Ravens. They beat the Dolphins pretty handedly at home in both of the team's playoff match ups in 2001 and 2008.

I believe that if a playoff team can win at home in the playoffs, it greatly increases the team's chances of becoming a Super Bowl participant. Home games should always be a team's competitive advantage. A team whose crowd plays a factor could in many cases, will the team to a home win.

Establishing a home-field advantage is crucial and, of course beneficial. There is a psychological boost that a team experiences when they have the confidence that they can win on their home field. A home-field advantage could also attract more fans that want to be a part of a raucous event.

The only way that the Miami Dolphins can get to that status of the stadium being filled with over 65,000 boisterous fans is when the team is able to win consistently and often. Dolphin fans will support a Dolphins team that is accustomed to winning. When I can finally see thousands of screaming fans in the stands at a Dolphins' home playoff game wearing white, aqua, and orange is when I will know that the team will have the potential to write their own narrative of glory.

Consistency in winning will eventually equate to a newfound glory. The Miami Dolphins could do that with the talented players that they have accumulated over the past few seasons. In my opinion, the Dolphins are a young and talented team.

They can definitely win with more consistency when the nucleus of talented players matures. The Dolphins' coaching staff has done a good job of coaching the young players that they drafted, as well as the young and talented free agents that they have signed. Personally, I believe that in life patience does pay off.

Dolphin fans have patiently waited for the Miami Dolphins to become not only a perennial playoff contender, but also a Super Bowl contender as well. Some have "jumped ship" from supporting the Dolphins. When the Dolphins become a perennial contender again, I predict that those fair-weather fans will be back supporting the team again.

Building a consistent winner takes time. The Dolphins have rebuilt the team fast. They fortunately did not have to take years to become in a position to win.

As a fan, I was surprised that the Dolphins were able to compete on a high level when coach McDaniel took over. If the team can continue to build upon the success of the 2023 season, then the Dolphins will finally be able to become a consistent winner. No one has to remind Dolphin fans about the team's struggles in the past.

Once the Dolphins win with consistency, all of those seasons of mediocre to sub-par play will finally be forgotten. It will be long overdue in regard to success when the Dolphins become a team that is recognized throughout the whole entire N.F.L. as a team that plays with consistency and effort. Usually, that equates to more victories.

First, the Dolphins must improve on their quick exits from the playoffs when they make it to the post-season. Teams that win with regularity have at some point, been able to overcome their playoff woes. The Dolphins must become focused on advancing past the first and second round in regard to playoff games.

Right now, the Dolphins are up against a formidable divisional foe, which has consistently shown that they are more than capable of taking over the division. If the team from South Florida wants to win with consistency, they have to somehow figure out how not to allow those teams to dominate them. I believe that most teams in the N.F.L. would like to keep the New England Patriots from gaining their winning momentum.

As I stated earlier, the Buffalo Bills are a team that is trying to establish itself as the team to beat in the American Football Conference. They have frankly had the Miami Dolphins' number over the past several seasons. The Bills must be beaten in order for the Dolphins to feel as though they are a team that has finally arrived.

In order for the Dolphins to arrive as a team of consistency, they have to stop settling for second-best within the division. Pursuing an A.F.C. East title and winning it with consistency will result in the Miami Dolphins becoming a team on the path to glory. I believe that the Dolphins are more than capable of making a new glorious path happen.

Continuity on the coaching staff and front office will definitely lead to glory for the Miami Dolphins. Successful teams do not have a high rate of coaches and members of the front office leaving the organization. The Dolphins should know all too well that a head coach who is able to patrol the sidelines for a substantial amount of time has a greater chance to bring the team to glory than the hiring of various head coaches.

When the Dolphins had one head coach for over twenty-plus seasons, the team enjoyed their most success. No team can have glory and honor when the coaching staff and front office is not consistent. My hope is that coach Mike McDaniel could become the guy who patrols the Dolphins' sidelines for many years to come.

Of course, if he is able to win with consistency, the Dolphins will continue to keep him as the Dolphins' head coach for as long as he desires to be the Miami Dolphins' head- man. From the Dolphins organization's perspective, they cannot be quick to fire the head coach if he has one or maybe two down years. I am fully aware that the N.F.L. is a league that is all about results.

If a head coach is not winning with consistency, then the owner and organization can decide to move on from him. Unfortunately, some teams feel that a change is necessary, and that is definitely within an organization's rights. A coach, who is consistently successful, in many instances, will not have to experience that.

The N.F.L. is a business that is filled with high stakes and pressure. Most fans only see the end result of a coach's preparation, which either results in a win or a loss. It requires special individuals to coach a team season after season.

My hope for the Miami Dolphins is that coach McDaniel and general manager, Chris Grier will continue to help the Dolphins improve and experience the glory that the team deserves. Professional football, as a career in coaching, as a player, and a member of the front office is never easy. There is always something or someone that could pose a threat to a team's continuity like a significant injury or retirement of a star player.

For many seasons, the Dolphins have not had the luxury of establishing glory. Honestly, the franchise has not only been searching for another franchise quarterback to led the team for 10-plus years, but it has also been trying to discover the next young talented coach. Hopefully, the Dolphins have discovered their 21st century head coach who could help the team have as much success and glory as their divisional rival that resides in the Northeastern region of the country.

There is great anticipation in the air for the Dolphins organization, and also many of the team's loyal and adoring fans. I am always reminded of the Dolphins' past glory when the team plays in their throwback uniforms, and the end zones and logo on the fifty-yard line is changed to the way it was in those former days of glory. This tells me that the organization is fully aware of its past success.

Every team has a past and a future. The Miami Dolphins' franchise past, no one can deny that it was special. Currently, the Dolphins could make the new era of the organization just as special and glorious as it was in the 1970s and throughout the 1990s.

Media and social outlets are now starting to discuss the potential of these young Dolphins. Does this mean that the Dolphins are on the glorious path? Well, as of now, the "jury is still out." There are several occurrences that must happen in order for the Miami Dolphins to enjoy glory in the 2024 N.F.L. season and beyond.

First, the Dolphins must remain healthy as a team throughout the season. Secondly, the new rookies that were drafted in 2023 have to contribute to the team in some way. And lastly, the Miami Dolphins cannot allow themselves to regress or finish the season worse than how they finished in 2023, which was not bad by any means.

The Dolphins should not only pose a challenge to the top teams within the A.F.C. East, they have to become both a nuisance and a threat. Psychological attitudes and mindsets toward those divisional rivals in regard to overtaking the division could be the key to whether or not a divisional takeover for the Miami Dolphins was a success. There is a certain type of attitude and mindset that winning teams have to have in order to overcome their nemeses.

One mindset that a team must have to overcome a divisional rival is that the division is theirs for the taking. The Buffalo Bills have become the front-runner within the division. From the 2020 N.F.L. regular season to the 2023 N.F.L. regular season, the Bills have won the A.F.C. Eastern division.

I will not by any means state that the Dolphins as a franchise has suffered as long as the Buffalo Bills' franchise because they have suffered through more losing seasons than the Miami Dolphins. So, realistically, Dolphin fans do not have as much to complain about like the legion of Bills fans. If Buffalo can be restored to its past glory, then Miami has just as much of a chance of having their glory restored, also.

For the Dolphins, it is not a question of whether or not the team can become competitive because that is not the issue at all. The issue for the Miami Dolphins is how they can win the big games when everyone is watching. In recent years, the Dolphins have not been able to win with any kind of regularity, games that are televised on primetime.

When the Dolphins were a glorious team in the 1970s and throughout the 1990s, they won the nationally televised games. In order to regain their future glory, the Dolphins must strive to play their best and win when all eyes are on them. They cannot play timid or bad if they want to regain the glory of success.

Playing well when it counts should be the goal for the Miami Dolphins. This is why it important that players who the Dolphins bring in and develop have winning mindsets and mentalities. One could conclude that the Dolphins are still a work in progress.

Are the days of glory ahead for the franchise from South Florida? Only time will determine if the Dolphins finally accomplished a restoration in glory. Now, my beloved Dolphins might or might not be able to experience glory in the next or following year. That is to be determined.

The pieces are coming together for the days of glory for the Miami Dolphins to return. If the Dolphins continue to draft gems in the draft, then I will not be writing as though the glory days are hypothetical. Instead, the future glory of the Miami Dolphins franchise will become a wonderful reality.

Coach McDaniel has gradually transformed the young and talented Dolphins into a team that has the potential to be good on offense, as well as defense. This is a far cry from Dolphins teams under previous coaching regimes. As I look at this new era of Dolphins football, I am extremely optimistic.

They have the players to help them challenge and eventually win the A.F.C. East for potentially several seasons. The Dolphins are drafting players who come from solid college football programs. I can continue to discuss the Dolphins potential for future glory redundantly, but what will really prove that the Dolphins have stormed back to glory is how the team will respond when they receive praise from experts and critics.

Presently, the Miami Dolphins have a promising future. Many in the media and around the N.F.L. are starting to realize that fact. The window of opportunity for the Dolphins to win is currently wide-open.

There are growing pains that the talented Dolphins must experience in order for them to transition from a team that is playoff caliber to a team and organizations contending for a World Championship in professional football. Winning is fun, especially, if it leads to Super Bowl victories. Every Super Bowl winning team had to start from humble beginnings.

Once the team that won the Super Bowl graduated from losing a plethora of games, they began losing less often.

One thing that is favorable in this present era of Dolphins football is the team's roster of players with an unlimited amount of talent. I am speaking of the mix of young and seasoned veterans who comprise the team. When it comes to the future glory of the Miami Dolphins, it is definitely attainable.

The N.F.L. is a league that is difficult to sustain any kind of prolonged success. Teams who can become successful for a plethora of seasons are in the minority. In order for the Miami Dolphins to capitalize on their opportunity to become a team in the thick of the playoff chase, they must have a sense of urgency. Once the Miami Dolphins are able to win meaningful games, they would have answered, "yes", to the question I posed about if the glory days are ahead.

CHAPTER 11
Memorable Wins

On December 25th, 1971, the Miami Dolphins played and won a game for the ages. Their opponent was the Kansas City Chiefs, who were the class of the old American Football League. This A.F.C. playoff game would ultimately go down as the longest game that was ever played.

The 82- minute game would have ended in a tie if it were played during the regular season. Sadly, for the local fans in Kansas City, Missouri, the classic game was a local blackout, and would not be viewed by the locals. For the fans around the N.F.L. during that time, this game would serve as a treat.

In the first quarter, the Kansas City Chiefs were the first to score on Hall of Fame kicker, Jan Stenerud's 24- yard field goal that made the score, 3 to 0. Also, in the same quarter, the Chiefs would score once again. They scored on a 7-yard touchdown pass from late Hall of Fame quarterback, Len Dawson to the eventual star of the game, running back, Ed Podolak, which made the score, 10 to 0, in favor of the Kansas City Chiefs.

Beginning in the second quarter of that seemingly never-ending playoff battle, the Miami Dolphins would commence to even the point total of the Chiefs. Dolphins' Hall of Fame fullback, Larry Csonka scored on a 1-yard rushing touchdown to come within striking distance. His score made the game 10 to 7, in favor of the Chiefs. After Csonka's score, the Dolphins would eventually tie the game 10 to 10. At the end of the second quarter, that would be the game's half-time score.

Once the third quarter began, the Kansas City Chiefs would become the first to put points on the scoreboard. Chiefs, running back, Jim Otis scored on a 1-yard rushing touchdown, which helped his team regain the lead. This made the score 17 to 10, in the Chiefs favor. During this epic contest, there would be three ties and also three lead changes by game's end. The Dolphins came back to tie the score, 17 to 17 on late Dolphin running back, Jim Kiick's 1-yard rushing touchdown.

In the fourth quarter, the star of the game, Chiefs, running back, Ed Podolak scored on a 3-yard rushing touchdown that helped the Kansas City Chiefs take their final lead of the game. The score was once again in favor of the Chiefs, 24 to 17. After the Chiefs' lead, the Dolphins would score the tying touchdown before the end of regulation.

Dolphins Hall of Fame quarterback, Bob Griese threw a 5-yard touchdown pass to tight-end, Marv Fleming to finally even the score, 24 to 24, to force overtime. Both team defenses produced turnovers. The Chiefs would turn the ball over four times, while the Dolphins turned it over twice.

This playoff game of the ages did not have a winner at the end of the first overtime. The Dolphins needed a second overtime to finally seal the win. Late Dolphin kicker, Garo Yepremian connected on a 37-yard field goal to finally end the longest game in N.F.L. history. Dolphin fans could look to this very game as the beginning of the Miami Dolphins Super Bowl appearances, and the team's launch from obscurity into the national spotlight.

I cannot ever discuss as a Dolphin fan a memorable win without discussing the Miami Dolphins first Super Bowl victory. This game was far from an offensive shootout and display. In fact, the game between the Miami Dolphins and the Washington Redskins would go down as the second-lowest-scoring Super Bowl to date.

The Dolphins scored a total of 14 points, while the team formerly known as the Washington Redskins only scored 7 points. It was basically a game that was dominated by the Miami Dolphins. Miami drew first blood in the first quarter when Dolphins quarterback Bob Griese threw a 28-yard touchdown pass to Dolphins wide receiver Howard Twilley, which would be his only catch of the entire game.

Griese and the Dolphins took that 7 to 0 lead with only one second remaining in the first quarter. Throughout the game the Dolphins' defense reigned supreme. The Redskins had a talented, feature, running back in Larry Brown.

Brown could not break away from the Dolphin's "No-Name Defense. Wherever Brown went, the Dolphins defense followed. In 1972, Brown was the Redskins' leading rusher with 1,216 yards.

His toughness as a running back helped him and the Redskins earn their first Super Bowl appearance. Going into that game, the Dolphins knew that they had to stop Larry Brown if they wanted to earn a Super Bowl title. Because of his tenacious running style, and his ability to break tackles, Brown made many defenses during that season look silly.

Also, the running back was 1972's N.F.L. Offensive Player of the Year, as well as the National Football Conference's Player of the Year. Although, the Dolphins finished the regular season and the playoffs leading up to Super Bowl VII undefeated, critics and experts predicted that the Miami Dolphins would lose their first game of the season with a 1- point loss. In the second quarter of Super Bowl VII, the Dolphins would score their final points in the Super Bowl.

Running back, Jim Kiick of the Miami Dolphins scored on a 1-yard rushing touchdown to complete the Dolphins' scoring total for the day. Neither team scored in the third quarter. With the game in full control in favor of the Dolphins, it seemed as though the team would record a shutout.

On the Dolphins' field goal attempt in the fourth quarter, kicker, Garo Yepremian tried to kick a 42-yard field goal. His kick was low and blocked by Washington defensive tackle Bill Brundige. Yepremian attempted to pick up the bounced ball after the blocked field goal by attempting a pass to star fullback Larry Csonka, who was also playing on special teams.

As Yepremian attempted the pass, the ball slipped out of his hand, while he was trying to bat the ball out of bounds. His attempt failed when the batted ball went straight up in the air into the waiting arms of cornerback, Mike Bass, who returned the fumble 49-yards for a Redskins touchdown, with a little over two minutes left at the end of regulation.

If that failed attempt was successful for the Dolphins, the game would have ended by a final score of 17 to 0, which would have matched the Dolphins 1972 overall record. Though a blunder occurred, this game resulted in the only perfect season in the modern Super Bowl era.

Rice Stadium in Houston, Texas was the site of the Miami Dolphins' last Super Bowl victory. Held on January 13, 1974, the Dolphins would face the talented Fran Tarkenton and defense of the Minnesota Vikings. Both squads would enter the ultimate game with identical 12 win and 2 loss records.

The difference between this Super Bowl and the previous one was the fact that the Dolphins were favored to win by 6.5 points. Though, the Dolphins were facing the Vikings' "Purple People Eater Defense", it was the Miami defense that gobbled up the Minnesota offense. Super Bowl VIII turned out to be a lop-sided win for the favored Dolphins.

For the Dolphins, it was a clinic on how an offense could capitalize on an aggressive defense. In that game, the Dolphins offense did many misdirection plays. It was because of those plays that the Vikings' defense could not pursue the ball in the way that they would have liked.

Miami's offensive line would block one way, and Dolphin running backs would go the other. This was a clever strategy that would will the Dolphins to their second consecutive Super Bowl victory. Dolphins' fullback, Larry Csonka ran the football like a man possessed, en route to receiving Most Valuable Player honors.

Csonka rushed for a then record 145 rushing yards on 33 carries. The eventual Hall of Fame fullback put the team on his broad shoulders. On the Dolphins first two drives of the game, Miami scored two rushing touchdowns.

Larry Csonka scored on a five-yard run to put the Dolphins on top. Halfback Jim Kiick, Csonka's running mate in the backfield, followed up Csonka's touchdown with a 1-yard rushing touchdown of his own. As the talented backfield of Csonka and Kiick scored those pair of rushing touchdowns, the Dolphins never relinquished the lead.

They (the Dolphins) would enjoy a comfortable lead for the game's entire duration. The team was clicking on all cylinders. On offense, the misdirection and power running game was giving the All-world Minnesota defenders fits.

In the second quarter of Super Bowl VIII, the Dolphins would tack on an additional 3 points, when Dolphins' kicker, Garo Yepremian kicked a 28-yard field goal. After his kick, the Dolphins would increase the led to 17 to 0. While the Dolphins were building a steady lead, the Minnesota Vikings could not answer with any points of their own to combat the Dolphins buildup of points.

By the third quarter, the game was out of reach. Dolphins' Super Bowl M.V.P., Larry Csonka claimed the game for good with a 2-yard touchdown run that put an exclamation point to Super Bowl VIII. His score would put the Miami Dolphins ahead, 24 to 0. That was the end of the scoring for the Dolphins. The Minnesota Vikings would finally score a touchdown in the game's final quarter. 24 to 7, was the game's final outcome, as the Dolphins would capture their second Super Bowl title.

Standing in the way between a Chicago Bears undefeated season and the preservation of the Miami Dolphins 1972 undefeated season was the 1985 Miami Dolphins. On December 2, 1985, the Miami Dolphins played in one of the franchise's most memorable games in its history. As a twelve-year old kid, I can vividly recall the anticipation of this important game.

The history that was on the line for both the Bears, and especially, the Dolphins was too important to deny. Although, the Dolphins were not undefeated going into that game, the Bears, on the other hand, seemed as though they would end the 1985 campaign with an unblemished record.

This game brought in many of the members of the 1972 undefeated Dolphins to the sidelines. I knew that the game was big when the game, which was held at the former Orange Bowl Stadium in Miami, Florida, was played before a full capacity crowd. In fact, the stands in the Orange Bowl were rocking.

Miami got off to a great start in the first quarter. They attacked that powerful Chicago Bears defense with quick, short passes. The Bears were known for their defense, and the Dolphins were known for their explosive passing offense.

In the first quarter of that all-important game for the Miami Dolphins, the team ended the quarter with a 10 to 7 lead. But in the second quarter, the game was blown wide-open when the Dolphins' offense scored 21 second- quarter points, while the Bears could only muster 3 points. Although, the Bears scored 14 points in the third quarter, and the Dolphins only scored 7 points, this would become the final quarter in which both teams would score.

There was a memorable touchdown reception by former Dolphins wide receiver, Mark Clayton that was a synopsis of the kind of night that the Miami Dolphins would enjoy that entire contest. Quarterback, Dan Marino threw a pass that bounced off a Bears defender into Clayton's waiting hands. Once the receiver caught the ball, he ran all the way to the end zone for a touchdown.

In the Dan Marino era, this game would become one of his signature wins. He definitely made the 1972 members of the Miami Dolphins happy. By game's end, the Dolphins still held the distinction of being the only undefeated team from week one, all the way to the last game of the season, the Super Bowl.

In hindsight, if the Dolphins did not defeat the Chicago Bears, 38 to 24, the Bears would have ended that season as the second team in the modern Super Bowl era to finish the season entirely unblemished, due to the Bears' 15 win and 1 loss season that ended with a Super Bowl victory over the New England Patriots, 46 to 10. Because the Dolphins matched up well with the Bears and had a great game plan, the 1985 Dolphins came to the 1972 Miami Dolphins' rescue. The game would ultimately be remembered as the game that kept the 1972 undefeated Dolphins' unblemished record intact.

Blessed with two talented running backs, the Cleveland Browns had a solid rushing attack. Earnest Byner and Kevin Mack were the Browns' two-headed monsters on offense. These running backs brought back that old offensive style of football, which was primarily running the ball on almost every down.

Both backs would rush for a 1,000 yards each in the 1985 season. The Browns would finish the 1985 N.F.L. regular season campaign with an 8 win and 8-loss record. Although, Cleveland finished with a .500 record, they were divisional champions in the A.F.C. Central division.

In 1985, the Miami Dolphins were coming off a stellar 1984 season, which saw them compete for a Super Bowl title. They did not have as many total wins as the previous season, but still the team had a solid record. The Dolphins finished their 1985 N.F.L. regular season campaign with a 12-win and 4-loss record.

That was and still is an excellent record, in particular, according to N.F.L. standards. The playoff matchup between the Cleveland Browns and the Miami Dolphins seemed like a mismatch. Miami was considered by many experts, a team that was poised to make yet another Super Bowl run.

Cleveland, on the other hand, was viewed as the young upstarts. Both teams on offense were polar opposites. The Browns preferred to beat teams with their bruising ground attack, whereas the Dolphins wanted to beat teams by the passing of All-Pro, quarterback, Dan Marino.

When the Dolphins scored the game's first points, I did not think anything of it. The score was 3 to 0 in the Dolphins favor. I can recall also how the Dolphins were heavy 10.5 favorites.

There was no way that the Dolphins could lose to an inferior team. Boy was I in for a rude awakening. After the Dolphins initial score, the Browns would go on a tear. They scored 21 unanswered points in the first three quarters of that playoff game.

While the Browns were scoring points, their defense was holding Marino and his explosive offense in check. Running back, Earnest Byner of the Cleveland Browns was running wild. He scored on a 21-yard rushing touchdown in the second quarter to put the Browns on top, 14 to 3.

In the third quarter, Byner was not finished. The running back ran past the Miami Dolphins' defense on a rushing touchdown of 66-yards. I still remember how nervous I felt when the Dolphins fell behind, 21 to 3.

Soon, after Byner's touchdown run, the Dolphins would play inspired football. Defensively, the Dolphins did not allow the Browns to score any more points for the rest of the game. Miami's offense came to light when Marino found wide receiver, Nat Moore on a 6-yard touchdown pass. Running back, Ron Davenport brought the Dolphins closer with a 31-yard rushing touchdown to make the score 21 to 17. In dramatic fashion, the Dolphins would take the lead and win the game for good when Davenport scored on a 1-yard touchdown that would be the game winner. Miami survived the Browns, 24 to 21.

Returning to the playoffs after a four- year hiatus, Miami entered the A.F.C. Wild Card game against Steve DeBerg and the Kansas City Chiefs. This Wild Card match-up, though low scoring, would have a dramatic finish. Just like the game that I just discussed, in this particular playoff contest, the Dolphins' offense struggled for the majority of the game.

Through the first three quarters of that 1990 playoff game, the Chiefs shut down the Dolphins explosive offense. It seemed as though the Chiefs would have their way. Thankfully, for the Dolphins the game was played in front of a home crowd at the formerly named, Joe Robbie Stadium, in Miami, Florida.

Sometimes, a team can gain momentum from the home crowd. For the Dolphins, they needed every inch of that crowd to eventually pull out a fourth quarter playoff victory. Chiefs, wide receiver, Stephone Paige had an outstanding game.

He caught 8 passes for 142 receiving yards and a touchdown. The initial score of the game came courtesy of a Nick Lowery 27-yard field goal that put the Chiefs up by a score of 3 to 0. After the made Lowery field goal attempt, the Dolphins answered with a made field goal of their own.

Dolphins' kicker, Pete Stoyanovich kicked a long 58-yard field goal to even the score, 3 to 3. After the game was nodded up at 3, DeBerg threw a 26-yard touchdown pass to Paige for the Chiefs only touchdown score of the entire game. This would put the DeBerg led Chiefs up 10 to 3, in the Chiefs' favor.

In the third quarter, the Chiefs would score twice on field goals. Lowery connected on a 25, and a 38-yard field goal to increase the Kansas City Chiefs lead from 13 to 3, to eventually 16 to 3 by the time the third quarter ended. Once the fourth quarter commenced, the Dolphins would tighten up on defense.

Then, Marino and the offense mounted a fourth quarter comeback. The Dolphins' legend would first toss a 1-yard touchdown pass to Dolphins' fullback, Tony Paige. Once the Dolphins were able to score, that made the score, 16 to 10, with the Chiefs clinging to a 6-point lead.

In the waning moments of the Wild Card playoff contest, high drama filled the stadium. Down 16 to 10, with a little less than 3 and a half minutes left in regulation, the Dolphins finally got in front of the Chiefs when they finally lead, 17 to 16. Star Dolphins' wide receiver, Mark Clayton scored the winning 12 –yard touchdown reception from Marino.

The Dolphins left enough time on the clock for the Kansas City Chiefs to score the game winning field goal.

Kansas City was on their way to a win when Chiefs' running back Christian Okoye took the ball 26-yards into Dolphin territory. After the Chiefs would receive a penalty for holding on the very next play, which would push the team back 10-yards, Lowery had a more difficult field goal attempt. In the game's final seconds, Lowery missed the 52-yard field goal that just fell short, as the Dolphins would seek out a hard fought victory in this exciting playoff contest.

Week 11 of the 1993 N.F.L. regular season was significant in both Dolphins history, as well as in the late great coach, Don Shula's coaching career. The Dolphins traveled to Philadelphia to play the Eagles. It was 61 degrees on November 14, 1993, when Shula made history.

Shula and the Dolphins came away with a record-breaking victory. This was the game that coach Shula broke the late legendary Chicago Bears coach, George Halas' record for most coaching wins in the National Football League. It was fitting that coach Shula won his record-breaking win with two backup quarterbacks.

When the Dolphins entered the 1993 regular season, star quarterback, Dan Marino was the starting quarterback. By the time that the Dolphins played the game against the Philadelphia Eagles, the Dolphins would have backup quarterback, Scott Mitchell as the starter. Mitchell filled in well for the injured Marino.

In the first quarter, quarterback Scott Mitchell got the Dolphins off to an early 6 to 0, lead. The Dolphins' defense held the Eagles scoreless in the opening quarter. Both teams in the second quarter would have three lead changes.

First, the Eagles would grab a 1-point lead over the Dolphins when Eagles' quarterback, Ken O'Brien threw an 11-yard touchdown pass to wide receiver, Calvin Williams, which resulted in a score of 7 to 6. After the Eagles scored their touchdown, the Dolphins took the lead with a touchdown of their own. Dolphins' running back, Mark Higgs scored a 1-yard rushing touchdown to put the Dolphins back on top, 13 to 7.

Once the Dolphins answered with a touchdown, the Eagles scored on another passing score. The same combination of quarterback Ken O'Brien to Calvin Williams connected on another passing touchdown. This time they connected on an 8-yard pass.

During this game, the Dolphins would experience adversity. Scott Mitchell, the starting quarterback for that game was injured. He would not return for the rest of the game's duration.

Shula had to win his record-breaking game in the same way that he had to win in his stellar coaching career. Dolphin fans would recall how the Dolphins won their first Super Bowl with a backup leading the team for the majority of the season. When starting quarterback on the 1972 undefeated team, Bob Griese went down with an injury, his capable backup, Earl Morrall stepped in to help the Dolphins win during Griese's absence.

For the Dolphins on that day in 1993, the backup to the backup had to help Shula pass Halas in coaching wins. Backup quarterback, Doug Pederson had to lead the Dolphins to victory in the second half of that game. He received help from the Dolphins' defense and special teams.

In the second half of that historical and pivotal game for Dolphins' coach, Don Shula, the Dolphins' defense held the Philadelphia Eagles scoreless. On special teams, Dolphins' kicker, Pete Stoyanovich converted two field goals of 45 and 46-yards to give Shula and the Dolphins, a historical win. It was only fitting that coach Shula's record-breaking coaching victory would come at the expense of a backup quarterback.

2000, was the last season that the Miami Dolphins would experience a playoff victory. The game between the Miami Dolphins and the Indianapolis Colts was an instant playoff classic. This was a Wild Card playoff game that would become an improbable win for the Dolphins.

In the first half of the game, it seemed as though the game would result in a home blowout loss. The Dolphins did not score at all in the game's first half. To make matters worse, the Dolphins committed three first half turnovers.

Dolphins' quarterback, Jay Fiedler threw three interceptions. When I was viewing that playoff game, I remember having two thoughts. My first thought was the

Dolphins could have been down by more points than what they should have been, due to how bad the Dolphins were playing on offense. The next thought that I had was the halftime score is only 14 to 0.

It was a tale of two halves for the Miami Dolphins. Their defense came up big. Indianapolis only scored three points in the second half, which helped the Dolphins offense.

The offensive star of that game was Dolphins' running back, Lamar Smith. He single-handedly put the game on his shoulders. After halftime of that playoff game, the Dolphins scored a much- needed touchdown.

Smith scored on a 2-yard rushing touchdown to help the Dolphins slice the Colts lead in half. It was imperative that the Dolphins scored in the third quarter because the score by Smith definitely change the game's momentum. Dolphins' kicker, Olindo Mare brought the Dolphins ever so closer with a 38-yard field goal conversion.

Mare's conversion resulted in a 14 to 10, Indianapolis lead. The Colts answered the Dolphins with an ensuing 50-yard field goal by Colts' kicker, Mike Vanderjagt. Vanderjagt's conversion gave the Colts a 17 to 10 fourth quarter lead.

That would be the Colts' last score, as well as last lead of the game. Needing a touchdown score to tie the game, quarterback, Jay Fiedler of the Miami Dolphins connected on a 9-yard scoring pass to Dolphins' tight-end Jed Weaver. Weaver's touchdown reception made the score a 17 to 17 tie.

What I took the most out of that Dolphins' playoff victory was the tremendous amount of mental toughness that the Dolphins exhibited. In the N.F.L., it is not always easy to mount a comeback, especially, if the team did not play their best. As the Dolphins sent the game into overtime, I was pleased when they won the coin toss, but when the Colts forced a Dolphins punt after a holding penalty, my enjoyment turned into concern.

After a missed 49-yard field goal by the Colts' kicker, which sailed wide right, I remember thinking that the Dolphins had "new light." The Dolphins made the Colts pay for that field goal miss. Dolphins' workhorse running back, Lamar Smith scored on a walk-off 17-yard rushing touchdown in overtime to secure a 23 to 17 Miami Dolphins win of improbability.

2018 did not yield to the Dolphins becoming playoff participants. The contest between the New England Patriots and the Miami Dolphins was played as though it were a playoff battle. This memorable game is arguably the most dramatic and exciting win in Dolphins franchise history.

The mighty Patriots went into that game in Miami not having any concern for entering the playoffs. Miami, on the other hand was battling for their playoff lives. Although, the Dolphins did not ultimately make it to the playoffs that season, the December 9th, 2018 contest with the rival Patriots provided plenty of satisfaction for the Miami Dolphins and their fans by game's end.

In the contest's first quarter, the New England Patriots scored first. Fullback, James Develin rushed 2 yards for a touchdown. His score put the Patriots ahead, 6 to 0.

6 to 0, the game's score, resulted in an extra point that was missed by Patriots' kicker, Stephen Gostkowski. This extra point miss would become an important factor at the end of the game. The Dolphins answered the Patriots touchdown with a 7-yard touchdown reception by former Dolphins wide receiver, Kenny Stills from former Dolphin quarterback, Ryan Tannehill.

In the second quarter, both teams would score at a frantic pace. First, the Patriots scored on former Patriots wide receiver, Julian Edelman's 2-yard passing reception from former Patriots quarterback great, Tom Brady. Not long after the Patriots score, the Dolphins matched the score with a

54-yard touchdown run by former Dolphins running back, Brandon Bolden.

Bolden's touchdown run put the Dolphins ahead by the score of 14 to 13. A few minutes later, the Patriots scored on a 37-yard passing touchdown from Tom Brady to former Patriots wide receiver, Cordarrelle Patterson. After some time elapsed in the game's second quarter, running back, Brandon Bolden, formerly of the Miami Dolphins scored his second touchdown of the game with a 6-yard touchdown run to put the Dolphins in the lead, momentarily, by a score of 21 to 20.

His touchdown score would not keep the Dolphins ahead for very long. Just a few minutes before halftime, Tom Brady threw a 16-yard touchdown pass to former Patriots tight end, Rob Gronkowski. During the third quarter period, the Dolphins would score the quarter's lone score.

Former Dolphins wide receiver, Brice Butler caught a 23- yard reception from Ryan Tannehill. The Patriots would tack on two fourth quarter field goal conversions with 32 and 22-yard field goals. Those converted field goals propelled the Patriots to have a lead of 30 to 28, then another lead of 33 to 28 with 16 seconds remaining.

What ensued after the Patriots made their last field goal would become nothing short of spectacular? On a play for the ages, the Dolphins scored the go-ahead touchdown when the Dolphins' last gasp for victory was answered after several lateral passes. The game ended with a 34 to 33 win for the Miami Dolphins when former Dolphin running back, Kenyan Drake scored on a 69-yard touchdown run, which began with a pass from Ryan Tannehill. The game would become known as the "Miracle in Miami."

Important regular season games are typically played in December. The 2023 regular season game between the Miami Dolphins and the Denver Broncos was a game that every Dolphin fan viewing the game would always savor.

The Dolphins scored the third most points in N.F.L. history, with a 70-point scoring effort. On September 24, 2023, the Dolphins were on fire. They embarrassed the Sean Payton led Broncos. I am aware that it is difficult to score in any game, but no one could have imagined that on that day, a franchise record would occur.

This game came down to execution. Dolphins' quarterback, Tua Tagovailoa played his best game for the Dolphins. Tagovailoa was sharp. By games end, the quarterback's statistics would be outstanding.

Tagovailoa completed 25 out of 28 passes. He threw for 376 passing yards, while also throwing 5 touchdown passes. The quarterback looked poised and consistent on that sunny day in Miami.

Although, I eventually saw the replay of the game, when the game was live, I can recall looking at the box score on my phone. In the fourth quarter, I remember seeing the Dolphins compile 63 points. When I saw the Dolphins score that many points, I knew that a scoring record would ensue.

Years ago, the most points I saw the Dolphins score was 52 points when Dan Marino was the quarterback. The 70-point score was a shock, but it also allowed me to view the 2023 Miami Dolphins as an aerial circus. Even Marino, Duper, and Clayton when they played did not put up that many points on the scoreboard, the most they put up as a trio was 51 points, which was an overtime loss to the New York Jets in the 1986 season.

The most points the Dolphins scored in the Marino-led era, 52 points, was way back in 1995 in the season opener against the New York Jets. If the scoring of 70-points is any indication of a revival in the Miami Dolphins offense, then brighter days are coming.

This book is for the true DOLPHINS FAN. I have written this book as an optimistic, but honest perspective from the eyes of a life-long Dolfan. Hopefully, the Miami Dolphins will continue on their upward trajectory of being a franchise of football prosperity and success.

As a Dolphins fan, potential has been a recurring word and theme to describe the franchise for many years. Patience is a virtue and word that fans of the Miami Dolphins such as myself have not had a choice but to practice as a result of the franchise's struggles of acquiring the winning formula in becoming victorious when the games really matter.

No one can do anything about past history, but learn from it, whether it is good or bad. Miami Dolphins fans who are fifty years of age and older remember how classy the organization was and is in victory and defeat. On one or more glorious Sundays in February in the future, it would be a wonderful and exciting for all Miami Dolphin fans all around the world to finally utter after a Super Bowl victory, "PHINS UP!"

www.ingramcontent.com/pod-product-compliance
Lightning Source LLC
LaVergne TN
LVHW021237080526
838199LV00088B/4552